Copyright 2014 *Paul Gillespie and Thomas J. Barker, Jr.*

www.BaltimoreHomeBook.com

## Table of Contents

**Chapter One:** Do THIS To Have Great Showings And Get "Top Dollar" For Your Home — 4

**Chapter Two:** You Only Get One Chance To Make A First Impression: The Absolute Importance of CURB APPEAL (And Why Your Home Is More Likely To Sell If It Doesn't Smell Like Garbage and/or Feces) — 12

**Chapter Three:** Don't Even THINK About Hiring A Real Estate Agent Until You've Read This Chapter…..Twice. — 24

**Chapter Four:** What You Need To Know Before Listing Your Home — 38

**Chapter Five:** How To Sell *Luxury* Homes (The Psychological Reasons Why $300,000+ Listings Require A Completely Different Marketing Strategy) — 72

**Chapter Six:** The Fifteen Most Costly Mistakes Made By Homebuyers (And How To Avoid Them!) — 91

**Chapter Seven:** Dos and Don'ts for Choosing The Real Estate Agent That's Right For *You* — 175

**Chapter Eight**: First-Time Homebuyer? Six Things You MUST Do (That Most First-Time Homebuyers Completely Ignore)     194

**Chapter Nine:** Should You Sell Your Home Without An Agent? Insider Tips For Marketing Your Home As A "For Sale By Owner"     207

**Chapter Ten:** Titles, deeds, abstracts......*wait, what?* This Is The "Boring" Chapter Most People Will Ignore......That May Cost Them Hundreds Of Thousands Of Dollars     214

*Chapter Eleven: BONUS CHAPTER:* Think Your House Is Ready For The Market? Here's Why "Staging" Will Help Your Home Sell Faster.......For A Higher Price!

# 1. Do THIS To Have Great Showings And Get "Top Dollar" For Your Home

What we're about to tell you is uncomfortable for some people to hear.

We don't really know why, but for some reason, it's just really hard for some people. Even though it's common knowledge, and frankly, *common sense*, many people selling their homes completely ignore this. It's not that us Baltimore folk are unique. This is a trend seen across the country.

It's almost mind boggling as a real estate agent to see this over and over and over again. Well, "frustrating" is probably the right word.

Sellers who ignore the advice in this chapter consistently get less for their home than they otherwise would, and SHOULD, get. In fact, one of the easiest ways to ensure your home sells for less money--**or doesn't sell at all**--is to ignore this chapter. So.......please do not!

Alright, let's cut to the chase.

We know you love having the "art work" your children created at the Arbutus Arts Festival plastered all over your refrigerator, but to be honest, the buyers really don't.

And when it comes to selling ANYTHING (not just real estate) it's the buyer that matters. Not the seller.

You need to completely DECLUTTER and DEPERSONALIZE your home. All of the things that make your house a "home" need to go! We know this is blunt advice, maybe even a little rude, but we've gotta say it. We know many real estate agents out there are *thinking* it, but some are too timid to tell their clients the truth.

It is what it is. If you don't depersonalize and de-clutter your home, you might as well not list it!

Again, we apologize if we sound cranky. We're not. In fact, today is a great day! *(We are currently sitting at the Rusty Scupper watching the boats sail by.)*

**Let's get into specifics.**

The fridge is just *one* area that we see "decorated" that shouldn't be.

Now that we are discussing the kitchen, if you have any small appliances sitting out, put them in a cupboard! We know you use your toaster daily, as well as some other items, but if whatever it is doesn't look good in a photo……..put it away.

And that goes for the rest of the "stuff" in your house

home you want to be able to see it without it being packed with people, and you also want to be able to speak freely. This is difficult when the seller is still there. Back to the story.

This home had A LOT of stuff in it. We mean a lot. But let's get back to the body count. So are you counting? Owner plus three kids is 4. Keep that in mind. Then there was Paul and his two clients. That is three. 3+4 is 7 people. That's right, seven people in a 1500 square foot home! Needless to say, it did not show well for this reason.

Unfortunately, the people were simply a nuisance compared to the condition of the home. When they were walking to the front door Paul and his clients could smell the ammonia of animal urine in the home. They powered on. After dodging the 4 extra bodies in the home, they rounded the corner to find 3 dogs and 4 cats. (Keep in mind, Paul is a dog lover; he has 2 dogs that he loves very much.) One of the dogs was relieving himself of his last meal, on the carpet, in the family room. After noticing that, Paul scanned the rest of the room. There were piles of animal feces and urine everywhere like land mines in a field. So as this all starts to register in his brain, imagine the Jason music. Wheet, wheet, wheet, wheet. Ha Ha. Paul was immediately distracted from that by the burning sensation in his gut, followed by the feeling he was about to lose his lunch, and contribute to the soiled mess on the carpet. Paul excused himself from the home, ran around the side, and got sick in the bushes. His clients followed him outside having the same feeling. When they got to the car, they proceeded to douse themselves with hand sanitizer, in an attempt to get the smell of the house off of them! Needless to say, they didn't even get to look at the whole home.

Here's the moral of the story: if you want to sell your home for top dollar, DEPERSONALIZE and DECLUTTER.

Oh, and keep the poo on the carpet to a minimum.

**Let's get into specifics....**

Family photos...touchy subject. It's OK to have a couple family photos out, but when your entire house looks like a shrine.......you need to tone it down.

It's really difficult for buyers to picture themselves in a home when at every turn, they are seeing 11X13 framed photos of all 6 children from birth through 12th grade. *(Really--I have actually seen that! – Paul)*

Oh, and collectible. Knick knacks. Can't forget those!

Tom once ran across a "Gnome" collector. No joke! This person had every shelf and every cupboard full of gnomes.

Honestly, this person had lined up every open space of each and every wall throughout the entire house with gnomes. *(I couldn't even concentrate on my pre-qualification paperwork! – T.J.)* Gnome nightmare!

**Every size and color ever created. It was actually a bit frightening.**

Nothing against gnomes.....we don't care if it's gnomes, Precious Moments, model planes, autographed baseballs, or wine bottles. PACK THEM UP!!

Oh, and speaking of packing up. Your garage shouldn't serve as a "catch all."

If you haven't used something in a year, *get rid of it.*

Here's a classic story: We were touring a house and was pleasantly surprised at how hard the sellers had worked to get it ready to place on the market.

Then we go into the garage.

No wonder their cars are in the driveway! Is the floor dirt, or concrete, or what? I don't know because I can't see it!!!

That's when we heard this, "Well, when we bought new furniture 10 years ago, we saved this so when our son goes to college...."

Their son was two years old!

Another good one is, "Well, Uncle Frank passed away a few years back and we inherited his stuff. We just haven't had time to go through it yet."

GIVE

IT

UP.

Chances are that your kids won't like it or want it! Give it to someone who can actually use it. There are a lot of organizations out there that would be happy to take it. Let them!

Clutter doesn't just apply to the house. *It also applies to outdoor spaces.* We'll get to that in the next chapter.

## 2. You Only Get One Chance To Make A First Impression: The Absolute Importance of CURB APPEAL (And Why Your Home Is More Likely To Sell If It Doesn't Smell Like Garbage)

You've probably heard the expression "curb appeal" before. It's not some secret marketing strategy used by realtors. Everybody knows about curb appeal. But most people do NOT realize just *how* important it actually is.

Advertising gurus say that the headline is the most important part of the ad. Why? Because if the headline doesn't grab your attention, you won't read the rest! You have to get people to read the headline first. Real estate is no different.

Your curb appeal is your "headline."

You are selling not just your house, but the land it sits on also. If you think cleaning out your garage means "place it alongside the house," you couldn't be more wrong.

Pulling up to a house that has either a car collection in the driveway, old couches or other old furniture stacked up behind it, and/or poopy diapers on the front lawn, greatly takes away from the curb appeal. Trust us on this one.

One more story.

Here's one of our favorites: Paul was showing a house in Ellicott City in late May, but the bright orange pumpkin lawn and leaf bags still adorn the house as if those bags are an artful piece of landscaping.

Not so much.

Seriously folks, Halloween was seven months ago! Are you that lazy where you're not willing to spend ten minutes cleaning up the yard to boost the curb appeal? This could mean thousands of dollars in the final sales price, because it directly affects the *emotionally-driven* **perceived value.**

Remember, most people start their home search on the Internet. If your house is not appealing *outside*, chances are they won't go *inside*. It's like going fishing without bait....you probably won't catch much fish.

Another thing to remember on the outside is the *not-so-pleasant* subject of pet waste. Some surprises are good, but when you step in a pile of doggy doo doo on a hot summer day, it's not so good. That person will probably not buy your house.

Seriously people, this is not a war zone. If a buyer has to

dodge the bombs as if walking through a live minefield, it might be time to clean up the yard.

When it comes to cleaning and/or organizing, **put it on the top of your priority list.** If you don't have time, get less sleep! It's really that important.

If you can't find the time to clean your yard when you are trying to sell your home, either hire it out, bribe a friend, or make one of your adoring teenaged children do it. (That's what we recommend.) The child learns that sometimes you have to do things that are a bit crappy. (Crappy, get it?) So, life lesson for the youngster and poop free yard for the parent. Win-win.

Let us ask you this: **if you are in the market for a new car,** how impressed would you be if there were empty fast food bags, containers of half eaten fries, gum wrappers, and some dirty laundry inside? Car dealers would NEVER put a car on the for sale lot until it was completely clean and detailed. They often pay professional cleaners to make sure it's spotless!

Its standard in the car industry to make sure the product is clean. And, well, it's standard in **pretty much every other industry, too.** When was the last time you went to the mall and there was garbage in a retail store? It would be laughable.

When we buy stuff, we expect it to be clean. It's not a

nice extra, or a bonus. It's the price of entry. It's *expected.*

Here's what we're getting at: People are SHOPPING when they tour your home! If retail stores maintain an immaculate level of cleanliness to sell $30 shirts, shouldn't you present your home with an equal attention to detail? After all, most homes are a few hundred thousand dollars. Or more!

**When you stop and think about it, it's crazy that anyone would buy a home that wasn't absolutely spotless.** We would go as far as to recommend hiring professional cleaners if you *really* want your home to sell quickly. It *does* make a difference in how well your home "shows."

And while we're on the topic of cleaning, can we talk about another un-pleasantry?

Odor.

It may seem strange, but many people put a name on each house they see, to help them remember it. And it usually has to do with the smells.

Paul still talks about showing the hamster house, the cat house, the candle house, the creepy doll head house, the pee house and the famous GARBAGE HOUSE! This one rivals the "Animal bathroom" house we wrote about earlier.

The "garbage house" was located in Dundalk. When Paul pulled up it was not too bad on the outside. It needed a bit of cleaning, but the potential was there.

However, when he opened the door, he turned and RAN back to the car!

The house had been vacant for over a month and the garbage was not taken out. Not only that, but they left the freezer full of meat, and the power had gone out. The owners must have been hoarders of sorts. It was bad!

Yikes.

There are no words to describe what those smells were like. Let me just say that no one was in the mood for lunch after looking at that house!

**When it comes to human memory, guess which of the five senses is strongest?** Yep---smell!

Scientists have documented that smells send powerful signals to the memory center of our brain, the hypothalamus. In fact, the olfactory system (fancy word for "sense of smell") is part of the brain's *limbic system*. The limbic system is responsible for memories and emotions.

When you smell a new scent for the first time, you link it

to an event, a person, a thing, or even a moment. Your brain forges a link between the smell and a memory -- associating the smell of chlorine with summers at the pool or hot dogs with baseball games, etc.

When you encounter the smell again, *the link is already there*, ready to evoke a memory or a mood.

**What does this mean for you as a home seller?** People will REMEMBER what your house smells like. Because of its location in the brain's limbic system, smell evokes strong *memories* and *emotions*.

If you're trying to sell your home for top dollar, even the slightest unpleasant odors can ruin a potential sale.

Unpleasant smells can ruin an otherwise lovely home! That being said, your home can smell great, but if it hasn't been updated since the Carter administration, well, don't expect to get top dollar.

Or any dollar.

So there's what NOT to do. But here's something you've probably heard before that you *should* do. And if you haven't already, what are you waiting for?!

Here it is: a little paint goes a LONG way!

**Fresh, neutral paint is the most inexpensive way to boost the value of your home.** Period.

You may think little Johnny's finger painting is cute on the wall, but the buyers will beg to differ.

Over time, you have probably changed your artwork around, moved furniture around, and maybe (probably) accumulated some scratches or other "wall injuries."

The sponge paint house...Yup, a house that will forever be dubbed that. We don't just mean the interior. We mean the exterior. All of it.

Let us tell you a basic rule of thumb...

If you drive around your city, look on the internet, or get ideas from Pinterest, *and don't see anything remotely close to what you're thinking of for a paint scheme*, don't do it.

Different is fine *if you are staying in your home.* Go for it.

If you're selling, it is not the time for daring or to be different!!! If you have old awnings, remove them. Old faded shutters - either paint them, or remove them. Sometimes it's as simple as getting out the pressure washer.

Spiders, dirt, and general uncleanliness can make your

house look neglected. Remember: your home should be SPOTLESS before selling. Not "clean" in a general sense, but *spotless*. You know, able to pass a "white glove test."

We'll again return to the car metaphor: Your home should be as clean as a brand new car. Even if it was built in the 1940's, it should at least *feel* like a new home.

It's a PRODUCT, and you are displaying it!

You've probably heard the quote, "It's the little things." What we have discussed so far has not been expensive big-ticket items, but maintenance items. It all matters!

We know, we know.......it's hard to objectively look at your home from the perspective of a buyer, **but that is exactly what you need to do.** And this is why many listings sit on the market for months and months, sometimes even having a birthday.

**Newsflash**: your home should not have a "for sale" birthday. If it's been on the market for an entire year, it's time for a change!

In general, a home should never take more than 90 days to sell. If it hasn't had multiple showings, inquiries, and offers before 90 days, something is wrong (Usually, this means it's overpriced, but there can be a variety of factors at play).

Again, this is *general* advice. In some markets and neighborhoods, demand is simply lower, and a house might sit for 150 days. It all depends on supply and demand, and how long you are comfortable waiting. Or, how long you can *afford* to wait for your home to sell.

What many sellers don't realize is the more DOM a home racks up (agent lingo for "days on market"), the more its reputation begins to suffer. Most buyers will become suspicious if a home has been on the market for a long time. They'll subconsciously think something is horribly wrong with it, or that the home is extremely overpriced (even if it is only *slightly* overpriced). Don't let this happen to you!

That's when you need a **brutally honest** agent (or a trusted friend) to walk through your home as if they were purchasing it.

When they pull into the driveway, does it look inviting? Is the grass armpit high? Is your trash bin overflowing in the driveway? Are there flower pots full of dead flowers--or worse yet--sun faded, plastic flowers? Upon walking in the door, do you smell a nice scented candle? Or do you smell a cat box?

Oh, and speaking of bad smells, make sure your toilet is flushed. Yeah, we know what you're thinking: *Roger that, Captain Obvious. Duh!*

Well, you'd be surprised....

Paul and his team have shown properties where bathrooms have not been checked. And that's a euphemism for "toilet was not flushed, and the sellers ate their vegetables last night." Not a good gift to leave for potential buyers.

Another thing I can't stress enough is *valuables*. PLEASE, for your sake and the sake of the agent, put them away.

**This actually happened to a For Sale By Owner (FSBO) that T.J. worked with on financing:** They were showing their own house. The parents kept them busy in the living room while their teenage daughter went to use the restroom. That is NOT where she went. She thought it took a little too long, and they left in a hurry. They quickly ran into the bedroom and noticed their *mother's diamond ring was missing from the dresser.*

She quickly ran out after them and asked them to have their daughter empty her pockets. Luckily, they (very reluctantly) cooperated and she got her ring back.

They never contacted her again and as she learned, they didn't use their real names when they looked at the house. Fortunately, nowadays, agents pre-qualify their buyers and generally get a bank letter so their identity is not so easy to forge.

And that brings us to another important issue: make sure the agent showing your house has actually "qualified" their buyers. There are documented stories about agents who were attacked, or houses that were scoped out during a showing-- only for the "buyer" to go back to the property later and help themselves to televisions, jewelry, and more.

We are not saying this just to fear monger. It is a real, documented problem.

How does that make you feel about selling yourself as a "for sale by owner?"

Again, we're not trying to scare you. But you do need to be aware of potential risks of letting strangers into your home!

And speaking of doing things yourself, if you're not qualified......*don't.*

That also holds true for hiring the least expensive guy for the job. You usually get what you pay for.

**Another nightmare story that actually happened to...you guessed it, Paul! (We're going to let Paul share this story from his point of view)**

*"We have a home in Abingdon MD. It was completely builder grade paint. Not nice, but can-live- with- it kind of*

paint. I mean straight up flat white paint that every particle of dust in the universe sticks to. Once the particle of dirt sticks to the wall, it never goes away. THAT kind of paint!

So my wife, being the go getter that she is, says, "Hey, paint is cheap. Let's do it ourselves." BIG MISTAKE! The first color she chose was red. Lip stick street walker red. I painted the backsplash and we went to bed. My wife, again being the go getter and early riser she is, decided to paint without me. Again, BIG MISTAKE!

I will not bore you with any more of the very comical few years that followed of us trying to paint. From the stair well feeling like I was painting the Baltimore Ravens football field, to again my wife decorating our carpet with a nice shade of teal paint that caused us to replace the carpets. Over the years we got better and better at painting but still not great.

Last year we listed that home for sale. It is a fantastic home. We moved out and then listed it. Guess what??? We did not sell it. Why you ask? I believe to this day that we STILL own that home because I chose to paint it myself instead of hiring someone who knew what the hell they were doing.

When my current tenant moves out I will have the entire home professionally painted so IT SELLS!"

# 3. Don't Even THINK About Hiring A Real Estate Agent Until You've Read This Chapter…..Twice.

Let's talk for a minute about real estate agents. Specifically, how to pick the agent that is right for *you*.

There is a sense of mystery out there concerning how the real estate industry "works." We'd like to shed some light on that. Before giving you our opinion (and some helpful analysis), we'd like to share a list of facts many people don't know about real estate agents and the "business model."

- Real estate agents are usually independent contractors, not employees.

- Most agents work on **straight commission.** They do not receive a salary.

- Most agents do not receive an advertising allowance, a client entertainment allowance, or an allowance of any kind. They pay for everything out of pocket.

- Usually the agent's broker takes a cut of the commission check. It varies from brokerage to brokerage. Sometimes it is a scale that adjusts based on how many homes an agent has sold throughout the year. For example, the more homes an agent sells, the higher percentage of the commission they keep. This means they make more "profit" (as a percentage of the commission) in the later months of the year. This is true for some, but not all, agents.

- As it is documented in many best-selling personal development books for real estate agents, **the easiest way to get rich selling real estate is to get as many listings as possible** (We'll touch on that topic later in the book.) *Sometimes this is at odds with what is best for the client.*

- Many agents also have to pay a "desk fee" (rent for keeping a desk in an office.)

- There will be additional closing costs above and beyond paying the agent's commission. These are always negotiable between the buyer and seller.

- Agents incur a lot more expenses selling (or helping you purchase) a home than most people realize. *Just one example* is the price of gasoline and wear and tear on a vehicle. When you're constantly driving to meetings and showing homes, the miles can add up pretty quickly!

*(Personally, I drive about 30,000 miles a year assuming I don't take any additional road trips or vacations out of state. With the price of gasoline continually climbing, it's a pretty major expense! – Paul)*

- Just as is the case in other professions, **there are different levels of certification and expertise for real estate agents.** For example, did you know that the term "Realtor" isn't merely a general term for a real estate agent? Achieving "Realtor" certification is the industry's equivalent of an accountant becoming a CPA, a financial planner earning a CFP designation, or a business professional getting an MBA. All Realtors are licensed real estate agents, but *not all real estate agents are certified Realtors.* There are a few other certifications, too: ABR, CRS, CRP, GRI, etc.

- According to the *National Association of Realtors* 2013 Member Survey, the median income for Realtors is $33,500. For the most part, real estate agents are not making big bucks. Exceptions prove the rule.

- They all have our listings on each other's web sites. The fancy term for this is "Broker Reciprocity."

- Any licensed agent out there can show any company's

listings--unless the seller doesn't want it that way (which is rare.)

- It will take a few hours for an agent to do the proper research and create what's called a "CMA" (Comparative Market Analysis.) A CMA is a report that tells home sellers what their home is worth, **and what price it should be listed at.** Some agents have fancy software that automatically generates a report by pulling data from the MLS. These automatically generated reports are usually very unreliable, as intangibles (things beyond square footage, number of bedrooms, comparables, etc) make a big difference. For this reason, Paul shy's away from being overly dependent on software. Each agent is different.

- There are lots of weird laws that prohibit agents from giving certain kinds of advice. For example, I am not allowed to tell you if a neighborhood is good or bad. I can't even say things like "Stay away from that neighborhood, there's a lot of crime there." This is called **steering**, and is actually illegal according to the *Fair Housing Act.* "Steering" applies to most qualitative questions: demographics of a neighborhood, quality of the schools, etc. Legally, all an agent can do is point you to websites that provide objective, hard data. In our opinion, this is a really stupid law. We completely understand the intent of the law (preventing agents from discriminating,) but it seems a bit silly. If one of us were a homebuyer from out of town, we would *want* an agent to share their opinion about these topics! We'll probably get in trouble for this little rant, but it's a common complaint amongst real estate agents. Everybody is *thinking* it, but we're willing to actually *say it*: good intentions, dumb law. We both have a reputation for being brutally honest, and our clients appreciate that about us. That being said, we're 99% sure we'll get in trouble for expressing our views in this paragraph. But you, dear reader, deserve to know the truth.

Now that you've got a crash course in the "business model" of real estate, let's dive into picking the agent that's right for you.

What we're about to say might offend some people, but it is what it is: **if you want the best service, hire a full time agent.**

It's pretty self-explanatory: full time agents devote their entire day to buying and selling real estate for their clients. It's not a hobby or a part time gig; it's their career. Full time agents spend at least 40 hours a week serving their clients. We've found it's typically 50-60 hours, even up to 70 hours during peak selling season.

Again, to be brutally honest, there is just no way that a "part time" agent who is trying to make some extra spending money will have the expertise and knowledge that a full time agent does. Do you really want to trust the purchase or sale of a $200,000 asset (or a million dollar asset, for that matter) to someone who is just *dabbling* in real estate?

Full time agents are immersed daily in the world of real estate. In fact, most full time agents we know don't even need to do much research to create a "market analysis" for someone wanting to sell their home—after a quick tour, we can quote a pretty accurate listing price. Doing the actual research merely gives us hard data to prove our estimate.

When you spend hours every day checking out the latest listings on the MLS, doing research on behalf of your clients, attending open houses, and researching comparables, it's almost hard *not to* become an expert on the local real estate market. The problem is that part time agents aren't doing all of the above. Or sometimes, *any* of the above.

**You should know that in the Baltimore area, there are a lot of part time agents.** If we were interviewing agents, we would make sure to ask them a simple question: "Is real estate your career? Is it a full time job for you?"

Especially around here, you'd be surprised how many agents are simply "dabbling" in real estate. They buy/sell a few properties a year. They're looking to make some extra cash. Earn a few commission checks, maybe a take a vacation they couldn't otherwise afford. Perhaps they're retired and just want something to do. Whatever their motivation, you should think long and hard before hiring someone who is "part time."

From our perspective, the "part-time" trend started in the late 1990's and 2000's as the housing market heated up. **During the housing boom, you actually *could* work part time and still make $40,000 a year (or more!) as a real estate agent.** That's on top of whatever you were earning at your "real job." With today's market, there are many *full time* agents earning that much. Or less. Oh how times change.

Needless to say, it was crazy. Word soon spread that real estate agents were making a killing (many of us were), and newly licensed agents started popping up like eager prospectors looking for gold.

Houses were selling like hotcakes—it didn't take much skill to show up to closings and sign papers! That may be an oversimplification, but it's not *too* far from the truth.

We think this time period is when people started to feel like real estate agents were making money *too* easily. And we can't blame them for thinking that.

Many homeowners started to silently wonder, "Wait, why am I writing you a commission check for $12,000? You hardly did anything to market it! My home sold in 8 days—that's $1,500 per day!!!"

Today, many homeowners are *still* skeptical about the value provided by a real estate agent (which is why more and more people are trying to sell their home as a "For Sale By Owner".) We think this skepticism is a holdover from the days of the housing boom, when, to be completely honest, *that skepticism was probably justified.*

During the 2000's, it wasn't that hard to make a good living (6 figures or more) as a real estate agent. Tom personally knew agents that got their license and within one year were making over $100k. Some of them did that in their first six months! There are not many professions where you can be a top income earner after one year on the job—and little to no training.

For the good part of the 2000's, the marketing plan involved three steps:

1. Upload new listing to the MLS

1. Place your sign in the yard

2. Sell it within a few weeks, show up to closing, collect commission check

It's not hard to see why people from all walks of life wanted to get in on the action! You could make millions as a real estate "investor" by simply buying a property in a nice area, holding on to it for a few years, and selling it after it had appreciated by 20%. This involved zero skill. *Anybody* could do it, and many people did.

It was like a game of hot potato—you just didn't want to be stuck holding an overvalued asset when the bubble popped. And eventually it did...

All good things must come to an end (for many of us who were personally *and* professionally affected by the housing bubble, we question whether it ever was a "good thing" to begin with.)

Without getting into too much detail, low interest rates driven by the federal government's housing policy created an environment where **everyone thought houses would keep appreciating at astronomically high rates.**

Keep in mind that historically, real estate usually appreciates at the rate of inflation (or a little more). If you look at long-term trends, owning a home is definitely not a get-rich-quick scheme. Unless, of course, you rode the housing bubble like a surfer on a good wave.

During the 2000's, homes were appreciating at 15-20% a year! It was chaotic. And it created a casino-like approach to buying homes. Housing in the 2000's was like the California Gold Rush. The amount of transactions taking place was *incredible*.

Because people irrationally believed that the appreciation was permanent and their home would continue to increase in value by 5-10% a year, they rushed to get HELOC loans (home equity lines of credit) to borrow against their equity.

**In a nutshell, people were using their homes as ATM's.**

If their home appreciated in value by $25,000 in a given year, they would immediately go out and spend that $25,000 as if it were real money they had earned. In reality, it was fake. It was paper wealth.

They used this money to go out and buy consumer products like boats, fancy cars, expensive vacations, new clothes, etc. This wave of spending gave our economy a short-term boost that made it *feel* like everybody was wealthy.

In reality, **the entire housing market was being subsidized by the federal government providing easy money.**

The housing bubble had nothing to do with actual supply and demand, and everything to do with the federal government's monetary policy. The government had spiked the punch, and we were in for a nasty hangover.

Seeing an opportunity for "easy" money lured many people into the real estate profession. They figured they'd get their license and get their piece of the action! And, well, we can't blame them.

During the housing boom, it was hard *not* to be making money as a real estate agent. New listings would sell in days or weeks—not months. It was super easy to get financing. RARELY did a deal collapse because of problems with financing. Banks were giving loans to anyone and everyone. Looking back, this was incredibly stupid, and a major reason why we had a boom and bust cycle in the housing market. As they say, hindsight is 20-20.

We've heard many people say that becoming a real estate agent is easy. And, again, to be honest, they are probably right. It's really not that hard to take the classes, pass the test, and become an officially licensed real estate agent.

What *is* hard, and what separates amateur agents from the true professionals, is dedication to the industry.

You simply cannot develop expertise or market knowledge by spending ten hours a week (or less!).

**Think about it this way:** would you want your family's finances handled by a "part time accountant" whose real job is not in accounting?

Would you trust your investments to a "part time financial advisor" who spends ten hours a week on the job?

Would you feel comfortable having your legal work taken care of by a "part time attorney?"

Would you be okay having a major operation done by a "part time surgeon" who just wants some extra spending money?

When the proper analogy is made, it seems *absurd*. (Heck, I wouldn't want my hair cut by a part-timer much less buying or selling an expensive home! – Paul) (I don't have enough hair left to cut – T.J.)

Now, keep in mind all of these professions require

proper licensing. Just like real estate, they do require official "certification." But just because someone is technically licensed doesn't mean you should automatically assume they are an expert! A piece of paper means they were smart enough to pass a test—it's *not* an indicator of true market knowledge, or wisdom that takes *years* to accumulate.

It might sound like we're bashing part timers. That's not the case! Some of them spent their lives in and around real estate, and now they are semi-retired (but still want to earn an income). Not *all* part time agents are inexperienced or lack market knowledge; however, it's worth repeating the question we posed earlier: would you entrust **the largest investment you will probably ever make** to a part-timer who is "dabbling" in real estate?

We mean, really, think about it--it's pretty crazy that people would trust a complete amateur to handle the process of buying or selling an asset that will cost *hundreds of thousands* of dollars.

Most people wouldn't hand over $20,000 to an inexperienced financial advisor, much less $200,000!

When you pay the agent's commission, you are not paying for their time to help you fill out the paperwork at closing. To be blunt, if you spent enough time reading the small print, you could probably figure that stuff out by yourself.

The *real value* provided by a real estate agent is everything that happens up to that point! That is where it is invaluable to have a true professional—an expert—working on your behalf.

# 4. What You Need To Know *Before* Listing Your Home

Let's get straight to the point: beware of agents that tell you what you want to hear in order to get their sign in your yard.

There, we said it.

We realize that we probably won't be making any friends by revealing this, but it needs to be said. There are agents out there who will list your property at any price you will agree to because they are afraid to be straight forward and tell you when the price is too high.

We apologize if you are a real estate agent and you are offended by the *truth*, maybe you need to do a little soul searching.....because chances are you are guilty of what we're talking about! That would explain your uneasiness. This is not always the case. There are some very good agents out there.

Now, to be fair, **this isn't some whacko conspiracy theory.** Sometimes what's good for the real estate agent is not what's good for the client. It is what it is. Nothing conspiratorial here. The same is true in *many* businesses.

For example, used car dealers want customers....but they also want to make as much money as possible. Someone buying a car wants to get a deal, while the dealer wants to make as much profit as they can. This isn't conspiracy, it's just the way it is.

What makes real estate **different** is that the process of buying and selling a home is much more complex than a $10,000 used car, so most people don't quite understand how it works.

And that's why we wrote this book!

Many folks mistakenly believe that their real estate agent always has their best interest in mind. It might *seem* that way (after all, they only get a commission if your home sells). But let's step back and look at the big picture.

Let's examine a transaction from **the real estate agent's perspective.**

Here's what you need to understand right away: the biggest problem most agents have is.......a lack of prospects!

Sure, a typical commission for a real estate agent may be $5,000 (or higher, obviously depending on the price of the home,) but that's *not* a lot of money if you're only doing four or five transactions a year. And many, many agents are trapped in this situation.

The reason it's difficult to make a good living as a real

estate agent is simple: lack of prospects.

And, to be fair, this problem applies to every business. I'm sure that car dealerships, appliance stores, gyms, movie theaters, lawyers, insurance agents, restaurants, and every other business out there would appreciate more potential customers calling them. The problem is certainly not unique to the real estate profession.

But here's why it might be a more "serious" problem for real estate agents: it's a feast or famine business. If you have a lot of prospects calling you, if you have multiple deals going on at the same time......life is good. In fact, life can be really good.

But the inverse is also true!

Most agents sit at their desks all day praying for the phone to ring. Hoping that someone will call. If you are a real estate agent scraping by month to month, every deal you are lucky enough to get is like manna from Heaven!

**You may go a month without making a single penny,** and then, *wham*! $6,000 commission check. Of course, your margin is eroded pretty quickly after paying desk fees, broker fees, advertising invoices, spending hundreds a week on gas, etc. But the point we're trying to make is that this is a feast or famine business.

Sometimes it's really good, most of the time it's really bad.

For most agents, it's a lot more like hunting than it is farming. Farming is predictable. Farming is consistent. Hunting is not. Hunters may go days, even weeks, before they get the big kill. But then they can eat for days and days. And rest a lot, because they are tired and their stomachs are full.

Like the modern day real estate profession, hunting is "feast or famine."

In our opinion, this is reigns true in Baltimore and its suburbs in particular. There is a huge influx of Realtors that are currently in the business or getting in the business. Most think that arriving in the business they will instantly make six figures and drive a luxury car. This is simply not the case. There is a saying that 5% of the Realtors do 95% of the work. Because of this, getting and maintaining your active client base is hard and EXPENSIVE! Most folks while very nice, will look out for their best interests at the end of the day. If an agent isn't committed to providing legendary Customer satisfaction, the Customer will go elsewhere.

With that being said, there is a lot of competition. Customer acquisition cost is through the roof. Other than the gadgets, the only thing that can set you apart from the next guy is good old fashioned Customer service. The only issue with providing legendary Customer Satisfaction is that it comes at a great cost to the agent and loan officer. We must be ready to work at the ring of our phone while eating dinner and trying to spend time with family and much, much more. We're not telling you any of this to complain. We love our jobs! We tell you this so you understand that our clients are our lives. They are an essential part of our daily lives. Not just work life because work and home are so intertwined. We are not playing golf every day or driving around in our nice cars. We are probably getting yelled at or walking through a pitch black basement with who knows what in there, because the client wanted to see the HVAC on the foreclosure they definitely are not buying.

But seriously, we can't stress this enough, we would not change this for the world. We take our jobs seriously. You (the client) are trusting us with your greatest asset (the home) and your largest debt (the mortgage.) If that isn't stressful, we don't know what is. It is stressful because we care. I am sure if you asked other great agents or loan officers they would tell you the same thing.

Now that you hopefully understand things a little better from "our" perspective, let us illustrate **what this means for *you***

**as a home seller.**

As we stated earlier, for most agents, real estate is a feast or famine business. Every listing they get, every deal they close, every commission check they cash is a big deal!

Here's an analogy...

If a small town used car dealer averages selling ten cars a month, it won't wipe out his business if he only sells nine. But if a real estate agent is selling one home per month, it can devastate them if they go more than a month or two without getting that elusive commission check.

Keep in mind that most agents have fixed costs every month that must be paid for (desk fees, cost of gasoline for driving their clients to check out properties, advertising expenses, etc).

When your income comes in lump sums (commission checks) and not a steady, predictable stream of weekly paychecks that most employees are used to, an interruption in your income can wreak havoc on your personal finances.

Trust us—we've experienced this ourselves!

That's another reason we're writing this book....it's a marketing tool that allows us to meet more people, get our names out there, and hopefully make some connections with potential buyers and sellers.

Now, for the reasons we just mentioned, it's VERY important for agents to have a steady stream of "leads." Because only a small percentage of all leads will ultimately become a paying customer that buys or sells a home, agents need relatively large numbers of prospects to actually make a sale.

You might meet with 5 or 10 people before one of them actually closes on a home!

Again, **we're not telling you this stuff to bore you**— you'll soon discover why this insider info is *very* important to know if you're thinking about buying or selling a house.

To summarize, real estate is a feast or famine business. It's unpredictable. It's tough being a real estate agent. Because your income is not consistent or predictable, it becomes extremely important to do whatever you can to *make it* consistent and predictable.

Trust us on this one—most agents will do just about anything to sell more houses.

**And from the real estate agent's perspective, you do that by getting more listings.**

Did you catch that? This is HUGELY important to understand.

The easiest thing a real estate agent can do to "hedge" against the uncertainty of an inconsistent income is…..get more listings.

Real estate agents *don't* get rich by selling a lot of houses, being expert marketers of their listings, having great service, a fancy website, or whatever else you may think contributes to success.

It basically boils down to one thing: <u>get listings, get rich.</u>

To be blunt, anyone who disagrees with this is either ignorant or lying.

There are DOZENS of personal development books written for real estate agents. Maybe even hundreds. One thing they all have in common is a "get listings" philosophy. There are usually entire chapters in these books devoted to teaching agents how to accumulate more listings. In fact, there are *entire books* out there solely about getting listings.

At this point you're probably thinking, "How does getting a bunch of listings help a real estate agent get rich? Don't you actually have to *sell* your listings to make money?"

That's a good question to ask. The short answer is "no."

<u>This is one of the biggest misconceptions about the real estate business!</u>

Many people mistakenly believe that agents are successful to the degree that they know how to properly promote a property, or how good of a salesperson they are. Other people will tell you it's "all about connections."

So there's plenty of agents out there desperately joining as many social clubs and organizations as they can, hoping to meet people and "network" their way to success.

This is all fine and great, **but what it ultimately boils down to is getting listings.**

I know, I know. It doesn't really make sense. After all, a used car dealer doesn't make money by accumulating a bunch of inventory. YOU HAVE TO ACTUALLY SELL CARS.

This isn't true in real estate.....

Here's why: as soon as an agent signs a listing agreement and places their sign in the yard, ANYONE can sell that home. Other agents have access to the MLS data, other agents can show the home to their buyers, and other agents can promote the home.

In fact, this is *usually* how it works. This isn't some weird exception or loophole in the rules. A vast majority of the time, a transaction involves a buyer's agent *and* a seller's agent.

In other words, the buyer and seller are *not* represented by the same agent. **Rarely does the actual listing agent find a buyer.**

What this means is that the commission is typically split two ways. The listing agent gets half and the buyer's agent gets half.

Because most of the "work" is done by the buyer's agent, collecting commission checks on your listings is *almost* a sort of passive income (**you should know that we'll probably get a lot of hate mail for the previous sentence, but it is what it is**).

Notice we said *almost.* There is obviously work involved in listing a home and marketing that home, but it takes much more time working with a buyer than it does working with a seller.

Reread that last sentence! We'll repeat it for emphasis: it takes much more time working with a buyer than it does working with a seller.

Phrased differently, earning $5,000 of commission takes a lot more time to earn if you're spending your time working with buyers than if you're focused on working with sellers.

Working with sellers is a "scalable" business model.

In this way, increasing your income as an agent isn't linear; it can be exponential. However, if you are working with buyers, there are only so many hours in a week. You can only work with so many buyers before you run out of hours in a day.

This is not true of working with sellers. Once they've listed with you and your sign is in the ground, you can start looking for the next listing…..and wait for another agent to bring a buyer for the last one.

Can you see how this creates a big incentive for agents to primarily pursue listings?

Oh, and did I mention that **having their sign in your yard is free advertising for the agent?** Newspaper ads in the local newspaper cost several hundred dollars per day. Billboards can be nearly $1000/month in prime locations. Radio ad campaigns cost hundreds of dollars per week. Sending direct mail is around 50 cents per letter. As you can see, advertising is EXPENSIVE.

Don't underestimate the value to the real estate agent of having their sign in your yard for a few months. It's free advertising for them! And having free advertising is a big deal with how expensive most media has become in recent years.

When an agent has their for sale signs in dozens of yards, it's like having a collection of mini-billboards all over town. Buying that kind of exposure would be *extremely* expensive.

This is yet another reason agents have an incentive to "get listings."

This means that ambitious real estate agents can *leverage their time* by focusing on working with as many sellers as possible. Which is another way of saying "getting listings."

When an agent focuses on working with sellers, they invest a little bit of time upfront in "getting the listing," then the commission checks come in weeks or months later *almost as passive income.* Almost.

When you work with buyers, you are constantly spending time with them, touring homes, meeting with them, driving around researching neighborhoods, helping them arrange financing, etc. Working with a buyer client is DEFINITELY not passive income for a real estate agent.

Don't misinterpret what we're saying here. **Getting listings isn't *inherently* a bad thing.**

But it can become a problem if the agent is getting listings *at the expense of their current listings.* In other words, it's a conflict of interest when they are neglecting proper promotion and marketing of their current listings so they can have more time to pursue additional listings.

Relatively speaking, collecting commission checks when you are the listing agent is passive income *when compared to representing a buyer.*

For most agents, their only time commitment once a listing contract is signed is calling to check in with the seller every week or so. Yes, there are open houses every now and then, but it's not like the agent is spending 2 hours every day on the front lawn jumping up and down waving their sign.

Working with buyers is *completely different*—it's easy to spend an entire afternoon with buyer clients, show them four houses, and not see any measurable return on that time investment.

Paul has had some buyer clients that he has shown over TWENTY homes to before they ended up writing an offer. We don't tell you this to complain about working with buyers....Paul LOVE's working with buyers. It's *fun*! House-hunting in real life is way cooler than watching "House Hunters" on HGTV ;)

**But you need to know the incentives this system creates for real estate agents.** On a per hour basis, it's MUCH MORE PROFITABLE to spend your time getting listings.

Allow that to sink in. We'll repeat it again for emphasis: on a per hour basis, it's much more profitable to spend your time getting listings.

You can't scale or leverage your business if you're spending all your time with clients looking to buy a house. Real estate agents know this, so the savvy ones spend most of their time accumulating listings.

As you can see, this isn't necessarily what is best for sellers. To be fair, sometimes it doesn't matter. In a hot market, as long as a home is priced correctly it will sell regardless of which agent that is listing it.

But you'd be shocked to discover how little time an agent spends promoting your home ***once they've got their sign in your yard.*** Once it's uploaded to the MLS, they don't drop everything they're doing and start promoting your home. They simply move on to the next listing audition.

Making sales is important in real estate—but most agents focus on *selling the seller* on why they should list with them. Unfortunately, the actual marketing and selling of properties takes a backseat.

**Most agents don't do much to promote their own listings**....because they're too busy promoting *themselves* trying to get more listings.

We joke that for most listings, there is a three part marketing plan:

1. Upload listing to the MLS

1. Place sign in yard

2. Wait for somebody to call

If you're religious, there is a fourth step. Prayer.

All joking aside, the actual promotion of a property is usually quite minimal. Selling homes is very different from selling impulse purchases like food or clothing. Usually buyers who are already researching will contact you about the property. Effective marketing of a property certainly helps, but most of the time a listing is bought more than it is sold.

Does that make sense? What we're trying to say is that usually a successful transaction is more about the buyer buying the house than it is the listing agent selling the house.

It's not an impulse purchase that can be influenced by shady, manipulative, door-to-door style sales tactics...."So Bob, would you like to sign the papers today or tomorrow?" You can't trick people with "closing" techniques in real estate—it's a big purchase, and it won't be taken lightly.

The tactics that work to sell small dollar items don't really apply in real estate. Sure, people's emotions come into play, but most people are smart enough to avoid spending $200,000 on a whim!

Again, we'll repeat: **a successful transaction is more about the buyer buying than the seller selling.**

This is one reason it's so crucially important to properly stage a home, fix what needs repairing, and price it right.

The greatest real estate agent in the world can't sell a home if it's ugly, broken, and overpriced.

We know, we know……*duh.* But you'd be surprised how many sellers blame their real estate agent for their home not selling……when in reality, the home was priced 15% above the market and needed $10,000 of interior renovations.

We could write an entire chapter about that, but let's get back on topic here….

There's an old sales proverb that says "Most people hate to be sold….but they love to buy." This is exactly what we're talking about!

Regardless of how effective an agent is at promoting and marketing their listings, it ultimately boils down to: *is there a*

**buyer out there that wants this home at the price I'm willing to sell it?**

If there is, that buyer will find out about the listing one way or another (this is one of many reasons that For Sale By Owner properties are at a disadvantage).

Now, you're probably wondering, "C'mon guys, I thought you placed a high value on marketing. It sure sounds like you're saying that marketing your listings isn't important."

All things being equal, the agent with a better marketing plan *will* sell more homes (to see Paul's marketing plan, check out [www.gteamsellshomes.com](www.gteamsellshomes.com)).

But here's the deal…..rarely are "all things equal." In fact, this is a *really* stupid expression, because things are pretty much NEVER equal.

There are all sorts of variables that can make a difference: price, days on market, motivation of seller, motivation of buyer, time of year, tax implications, relevant comparables, staging, economic conditions, etc. We could probably rattle off a dozen more variables that can influence a deal, but I don't want to bore you.

With that in mind, the point we're trying to make is quite simple: when a home sells, the deal often happens because the buyer simply wants to buy. NOT because the listing agent *sold* it.

There is a difference.

You probably think we're playing word games. But trust us; this isn't semantics. There is a big difference between a buyer buying and a seller selling.

Maybe an analogy will help.

Imagine you're waltzing through Target, looking for a new DVD that just came out. You ask a nearby sales associate where it is, and they tell you which aisle to find it in.

Did the employee really "sell" you something? Not really—the purchase was driven more by your willingness and eagerness to buy. You weren't really "sold" at all. It's not as if you walked in to the store intending to buy shampoo, and the sales associate gave you a sales pitch ending with a hard sell, and you caved in and purchased the DVD.

Another example: have you ever been to one of those timeshare seminars where they bribe you into attending with a gourmet meal and a moderately expensive free gift? *No one* goes into those meetings intending to purchase a timeshare!

But many do end up "investing" in the product being pitched.

These people truly are "sold." Because of an effective marketing strategy that persuaded them, they take action. The credit in this situation goes to the salesperson! They were "cold" leads, not intending to buy a timeshare.

**This is not always true in a real estate transaction.**

Don't misinterpret what we're saying—we're NOT saying that listing agents don't do anything. We're NOT saying you're better off trying to sell your home without an agent (FSBO.) We're NOT saying the real estate agent's commission is a waste of money.

Here's what we ARE saying: **a successful transaction is more about the buyer buying than the seller selling.**

Successful real estate marketing is more about optimizing the home so that buyers want to buy it, and less about pouring tons of resources into promoting it.

Phrased differently, it's easier to sell a great product than it is to skimp on product quality, invest those dollars in marketing, and attempt to sell a mediocre product with a large ad budget. See the difference?

Real estate agents understand this, the general public does *not*.

We'll repeat it again: **a successful transaction is more about the buyer buying than the seller selling.**

There's a reason that some agents have dozens (heck, sometimes more than fifty) listings at the same time……but it would be downright impossible to work with that many buyers at the same time.

There wouldn't be enough hours in a day, or days in a week, to work with that many buyers.

**Here's the dirty little secret:** once you've done the upfront work of "getting the listing," it's pretty easy to sit back and hope another agent sells it.

Easy, but not always ethical.

In fact, many agents (not *all* agents) probably put more energy and resources into getting listings than selling those listings. This is because they are still handsomely rewarded (with 50% of the commission) when another agent brings the buyer.

On a $200,000 home, the commission will be roughly $12,000. This means that the listing agent would collect half of that (six grand) when another agent brings a buyer.

**It's a much more scalable business model to simply rack up a bunch of listings and allow other agents to sell them.**

Some firms avoid this conflict of interest by hiring buyer's agents that work exclusively with buyers, and having marketing directors whose job it is to actually promote the listings. We have assembled a team of experts to market your home efficiently.

By avoiding spending time and resources promoting their "inventory," brokerages can focus on generating as many listings as possible.

That's how it usually works behind the scenes.

Again, we're not saying they don't spend *any* time marketing their listings. Just that it's much more profitable to get listings (not necessarily market them)……and you'll usually see that reflected in how an agent spends his or her time.

**But can you see how this is clearly *not* in the best interest of the client?**

This is different from other industries where you don't invest a lot of time or resources into selling individual units of inventory. However, with something as complex as a home, you need to become an expert on that specific property. It's not enough to be knowledgeable on homes *in general*.

As the listing agent, you need to know that specific listing inside out. You need to know its strengths, weaknesses, and how to answer questions, concerns, and objections. You need to become more of an expert on that home than the homeowner.

You need to commit to promoting each listing so that it sells quickly and for top dollar!

It's *not* the same as a car dealer having lots of inventory. In that scenario, buyers come to him. He doesn't go and prospect for buyers for the individual cars—he advertises the dealership itself.

Real estate agents can't (and shouldn't) do that—each of our "products" is unique. So, in our opinion, we should promote each of our listings as a unique product!

And THIS is where what's good for the real estate agent is *not necessarily* what's good for the client. It's not always a "conflict of interest," but it often can be.

Let's say you own a home in the Perry Hall area. After talking with a few neighbors, including some family friends that recently sold their home just down road, you figure that your house is worth about $300,000.

As it is for most Americans, your home is your biggest investment. You aren't really looking for a "quick sale" where you are forced to sell it below market value. You need every dollar you can get, and you're willing to wait for the perfect buyer who understands the true value of your home…..and is willing to pay you what it's worth.

After interviewing several agents that want to list your home, you decide on Bob. Bob seems like a genuinely friendly guy, and his listing presentation was very impressive. To put the icing on the cake, Bob convinces you that he could get you $300,000 for your home.

Here's the problem: the market isn't willing to pay more than $270,000 for your home. It's overpriced by about ten percent. This doesn't seem like a lot, but in Baltimore County homes that actually sell usually go for about 94% of listing price (or higher.) In some areas of the country, you can get away with overpricing a listing. Not here. If the home is priced correctly and shows well, it should sell for close to the list price.

**Most buyers don't want to risk offending sellers by offering what may be interpreted as a "lowball" offer**……even if the offer is actually fair relative to market value. Most people would rather pass on the home entirely than risk offending the seller.

By overpricing your home—even by a measly ten percent—Bob is virtually guaranteeing your home will not sell. In fact, it probably won't even receive offers.

Here's why Bob does this: HE WANTS THE LISTING.

**Bob is willing to fudge the numbers a bit to massage your ego.** He tells you *exactly what you want to hear*......that if you list with him, he can get you the $300,000 your home is worth.

Remember: you are not an expert on the local real estate market. You haven't spent hours researching comparables and creating a market analysis report. So what do you do? You listen to Bob. You trust him.

This is an example of "**confirmation bias**," a term in psychology that describes when people pretend to be objective. What's really happening is Bob told you what you wanted to hear, so you convince yourself that he's right. You didn't objectively analyze the situation; you chose to accept the information that matched with what you *wanted* to be true.

In this scenario, the brutally honest real estate agent that tells you the truth usually misses out on the listing.

When you hear that your home is actually worth $270,000, you don't want to believe it. Rather than confronting reality, what many sellers do is list with the agent that promises them the highest price. They don't know any better, so they substitute emotion for logic.

This dynamic can lead to some interesting listing presentations....

Oftentimes, the seller will get angry when you tell them what their home is actually worth. After all, the agent before you reassured them their home is worth *much more* than the number you gave them. By "lowballing" their home's value, you've insulted them.

Paul has seen this more times than he can count—but it comes down to integrity. We believe a real estate agent should tell you what your home is actually worth—not what you *think* it's worth. Or worse, what you *want* it to be worth.

Oh, by the way, Bob knew this whole time that the home was actually worth about $270,000....

**Here's another dirty little secret of the real estate industry:** creating market analysis reports is just as much art as it is science.

Sure, hours of research go into creating these reports, but the final recommended listing price is heavily influenced by the selfish motivation of, "Will this number make the seller more or less likely to list with me?"

Unfortunately, it's just a fact of life that human beings are narcissistic. We want to be told we're awesome. We want to be told our kids are awesome. And want to be told that our homes are worth more than they actually are.

Real estate agents understand this. Most sellers do not.

We call this technique *buying the listing.* It's unethical, but there's really no way of "proving" that a real estate agent is doing it.

Let's go back to the example of Bob.

Because Bob succeeded in appealing to your ego, he wins the listing. Bob lists it slightly above $300,000, telling you he hopes to negotiate a final deal of $300,000.

One month passes, and there has been two showings. No offers.

**The first month a listing is on the market is critical.** If you aren't getting immediate attention in the first 30 days a home is listed—phone calls, emails, showings, offers—something is wrong with the listing. Nine out of ten times it is overpriced.

Remember, Bob KNOWS it is overpriced. He quoted you a listing price that he knew was too high. After a few months of misery, Bob calls you up and tells you that, "The market has changed since we listed your property. Demand has dipped. Our original listing price is now too high. I think we need to drop the price twenty grand or so. If you are unable to do that, I understand. But I want you to know that with the current market conditions, I don't think your home will sell at the current price."

Bob will most likely quote you plenty of data to prove his point….

**This is a technique commonly used by real estate agents.** It shifts the blame from the agent to the market, so sellers don't get mad at the agent………when in reality, the agent *knowingly* overpriced the listing originally.

A month passes, and you wait it out. You don't want to "lose out" on twenty thousand dollars, in case the perfect buyer comes along and falls in love with your house. But that doesn't happen. In fact, this pretty much never happens.

So, after multiple months of your home sitting on the market, you reluctantly give Bob a call and give him permission to drop the price of your home.

*Voila*—it sells within two weeks.

Most people (not knowing that the home was originally overpriced) will credit Bob with "adapting to the market" and doing what was necessary to get the property sold.

What usually goes undetected is that Bob uses this strategy over and over and over again to win listings from more honest agents.

**Here's a breakdown of how some agents *buy the listing:***

1. Quote an inflated listing price to impress the sellers and get their foot in the door

1. Win the listing by convincing sellers the home is worth more than it actually is

2. Patiently wait while the overpriced listing accumulates "days on market."

3. When the seller's frustration reaches a breaking point, convince them to reduce the price (to the actual price it should have been all along)

4. Sell the listing months after it *should have* sold.

5. Repeat steps 1-5

This process is most easily executed when the seller agrees to a long-term listing contract. Sometimes it's as short as sixty days, but often the listing contract is 6 months or a year. Because the seller has legally signed a contract and cannot "fire" the agent, *they cannot escape without penalty*. The contract is what makes this underhanded tactic so effective—it doesn't really matter if the seller realizes he's been tricked, because the terms of the contract won't allow him to exit the agreement.

**Agents know this**, so most of them insist on the seller signing a lengthy contract.

*"Let me be loud and clear on this point: I DO NOT FORCE MY CLIENTS TO SIGN LONG TERM CONTRACTS. Period.*

*In fact, if a seller wants to fire me the day after they sign a listing agreement, I believe it is their right to do so. This incentivizes me to provide great service to all of my clients—if I don't, they can fire me with an email. Its that simple. To me, it's just common sense."* - Paul

This raises an interesting question: why do so many agents insist on the seller signing a long-term contract? Are they that scared of their clients firing them, that they feel it's necessary to lock the client in to a contract?

To be fair, we're not saying that all agents who use long-term contracts are evil. Not at all! We have *many* friends in the industry that use long-term contracts. So please don't take this out of context.

**Contracts are not *inherently* a bad thing.** It's when a

contract is used as a tactic to take advantage of sellers that it becomes a problem.

In fact, historically, using contracts is a pretty standard practice in the industry. Most agents (and clients) sign contracts without thinking about it, because that's the way it's always been done.

Now that we've exposed how some agents "buy listings," let's reveal how to avoid this problem. (This might make some agents verrrrrrrry uncomfortable....)

**There are two HUGELY IMPORTANT questions you should ask *any* agent that wants to list your home.**

First, "What is the average 'days on market' of your listings?" In other words, how long does it take you to sell your listings, on average? The answer to this question will reveal how quickly the agent sells their listings. Many agents out there can brag about selling the most homes in the area, or even getting "top dollar" for their clients—but it's all rather meaningless if it takes them 8 months to sell a home!

Here's why this is so important: asking the agent about their average *days on market* puts YOU in the driver's seat. You don't have to stress out about selecting an agent when you can *objectively* compare them based on hard data.

So feel free to ignore the fancy PowerPoint presentations, the glossy marketing literature, and the smooth talking sales jargon.

All that matters is the agent's track record of selling homes. And by that I mean *the actual MLS statistics*—not a vague reply like "Well I usually sell my listings very quickly!"

If the agent doesn't know their numbers (or refuses to give you this information), it's a pretty good indicator that you should *not* hire them.

In fact, many potential sellers are afraid of meeting with agents because they think the agent will give them an awkward "hard sell" they can't refuse. This is probably more of a problem in Baltimore....we are too nice to politely refuse.

Again, the reason it's important to ask this question is because it puts *you* in control. Buying and selling a home is probably the most expensive thing you will ever do—doesn't it make sense to do some research?

Because, let's be honest, the reason it makes sense to hire a real estate agent in the first place is because you (the seller) aren't an expert on local real estate. But this is a paradox for many sellers—if you *don't* understand the local market, how can you possibly make an intelligent decision when it comes to choosing an agent?

Just like any other profession, there are agents out there that can give an amazing "listing presentation," but fail miserably at actually selling houses. And the inverse is also true. There are agents that aren't particularly talented at wooing sellers, but are extremely effective at selling their actual listings.

So don't put too much emphasis on an agent's "listing presentation." Take control of the situation and request the agent's average DOM statistic as part of the listing audition.

**The second question you must ask is**, "What is your average listing/sale price ratio?"

The answer to this question reveals how accurate the agent is at pricing their listings. *A good ratio is approximately 94%.*

Anything higher than 94% means the agent is selling their listings very close to the listing price. This is a good thing. It usually will attract multiple offers and ensures the home sells quickly.

i.e., a 94% ratio means they are successfully selling $200,000 listings for $188,000.

Anything less than 94% means that they are chronically

overpricing their listings. The actual target ratio will be different for every market. We're speaking from experience in the Greater Baltimore area—around here, homes typically sell for about 94% of list price....so you need to have a pricing strategy that reflects that. In some markets it may be 90%, or even 85%.

**The higher a region's ratio, the greater the danger of overpricing your listing.**

Because listings in the Baltimore area *typically* sell for around 94% of list price, this means that overpricing your home by more than 5% will drastically reduce the likelihood of a quick sale…….or any sale at all.

If there is a large difference between what an agent's listings are *selling* for versus listed for, you will know they are playing the "buy listings" game. Either that, or they're too inexperienced to know what local properties are actually worth.

Both of these are reasons to *not* hire this agent.

Remember to ask these two questions when it comes time to "interview" potential real estate agents. The very act of asking the questions (even if you don't get straightforward answers) puts you in control of the conversation. When you take the initiative in the listing "interview," the real estate agent will think twice about trying to trick you with inflated numbers.

As they say, the best defense is a good offense!

And if you aren't personally selling anytime soon, *but know someone who is*, be sure to pass this advice on.

## PS

The hypothetical story of "Bob" found earlier in the chapter is based on a true story.

Paul didn't "get the listing" because another agent convinced the sellers their home was worth much, much more than it actually was.

It took OVER A YEAR TO SELL.

And, for the record, Paul tracked this particular home. He was curious what it would end up selling for. Over a year later, it sold within $2,000 of the original listing price Paul had quoted the seller. Go figure.

## 5. How To Sell *Luxury* Homes (The Psychological Reasons Why $500,000+ Listings Require A Completely Different Marketing Strategy)

It sounds obvious, but the typical advertising used to sell a $50,000 fixer upper will NOT work when marketing a million dollar estate in Hunt Valley.

Many people mistakenly believe that all they need to do is spend a little more money to promote a "luxury" listing. They'll keep the actual advertising more or less the same, but simply buy more ads. Or larger ads.

It's not that simple.

This isn't an issue of math, where you simply adjust the marketing budget to fit the listing price. Yes, you *will* need to invest more money promoting a luxury home. That's a given. Some agents fail to invest enough, which is their *first* problem. But it gets worse—some sellers make the wrong *kind* of marketing investments.

It's not as easy as taking whatever you typically spend on a "normal" listing and adding a few zero's.

If you want your luxury home to sell for top dollar in a reasonable amount of time, you can't settle for a difference *in degree*. You need a difference *in kind*.

We're talking about the difference between evolution and revolution. Evolution implies you make minor tweaks to something. Revolution implies you completely start from scratch with an entirely new paradigm.

Effective marketing of luxury homes requires a completely different strategy. Not the same strategy, with a slightly larger advertising budget. It demands an entirely new way of thinking. You can't just take the same advertising you use for "regular" listings, and buy larger ads.

We see real estate agents make this mistake all the time.

**It's unfair to the sellers, because it virtually guarantees that their listing will sit on the market much longer than it should.** And when a listing sits on the market for more than a few months, it begins to develop a reputation…..and not a good one.

When buyers and their agents find a listing that's been on the market for a long time, they usually throw out lowball offers. And we can't blame them—it's a fair assumption that a seller may be desperate if their home hasn't sold after 3, 4, 5 months (or longer.)

This creates a vicious cycle!

*It's even worse for sellers of luxury listings*, because instead of resorting to a price cut of $5,000 or $10,000, they often need to trim the listing price by $50,000 or even $100,000.

In fact, on high-end homes that have sat on the market for too long, we've seen price reductions much greater than $100,000! The higher the original price, the greater the reduction needs to be to stay competitive.

In real estate as in life, it's always in your best interest to make a great first impression.

And, like we said, this isn't an issue of math. It's about *psychology*. Affluent buyers who can afford high-end homes **think** differently.

*(In the Baltimore area, any listing higher than $500k counts as a luxury home, in my opinion. There may be occasional listings at or around $500,000 that are not "luxurious," but exceptions prove the rule. In Greater Baltimore, anything north of $500,000 is typically a newer, high end home or an older estate. - Paul)*

Because affluent buyers think differently, they buy for

completely different reasons than a typical homebuyer. Most homebuyers are concerned about details like utility bills and monthly mortgage payments. The luxury buyer does not care as much about these things. If at all.

The higher you move up the listing price ladder, the more important intangibles become. In other words, luxury homes are more about *art* than *science.*

On a typical $175,000 starter home, "the numbers" drive the entire process. The buyer closely monitors the potential monthly mortgage amount, the utilities, the interest rate, closing costs, etc. They are very much concerned with the "science" of the deal. They are restricted by the numbers.....their budget is the main driver of the process.

THIS IS NOT TRUE OF LUXURY BUYERS.

Now, of course, affluent homebuyers still pay attention to *the numbers*. They won't allow themselves to get "ripped off" and overpay for a home. That's how they got to be successful in the first place—**they are wise stewards of money.**

Instead of being limited by a strict budget, affluent buyers generally make their buying decisions based on a completely different set of factors.

Everyone makes decisions emotionally, but affluent

buyers can usually afford to ignore logic. And when we use the term "logic," we mean it in a strictly financial sense.

Affluent buyers looking at million dollar waterfront homes think in terms of $25,000 or $50,000 increments the same way an "average" buyer thinks of $5,000 increments. For example, a first time homebuyer might splurge an extra $5,000 to buy a home at the top of their budget if they really fall in love with it. The affluent buyer, who is looking at 6,000 square foot homes on the Chesapeake Bay , doesn't even flinch at an amount like $5,000. To them, "splurging" would mean buying something $50,000 over their arbitrary "budget." Or even $100,000 over.

The average person can't fathom increments like that—according to the US Census Bureau, the median household income in Baltimore is about $73,000 per year. That means the typical price reductions happening in our luxury real estate market are greater increments than what the average Baltimore family earns *in an entire year*!

This is why "regular" marketing strategies don't work with affluent buyers. You can't entice them with hypothetical "$10,000 off" coupons. They simply don't care about small amounts of money.

**Affluent buyers are much more concerned about finding**

**the perfect home than they are a home with the perfect *price*.**

See the difference?

To be blunt, luxury real estate has little to do with price. If an affluent buyer really, truly, wants a particular luxury home, they will pay almost anything for it. They want the perfect home, not the perfect price.

Affluent buyers are ruthlessly efficient in their businesses and careers *so they don't have to be when it comes to buying a home.*

We're not saying luxury buyers don't care at all about price. *Of course they do!* Most affluent households have an annual income of at least $250,000 per year. They are, if only in a technical sense, restricted by their budget. *But within that budget,* they have an entirely different conception of "value."

**They won't "overpay," but they *will* pay more.**

If you are not affluent yourself, the previous sentence probably makes no sense to you. If you *are* affluent, it makes perfect sense.

Buyers of luxury homes (again, we classify a luxury home as anything north of $500,000) have a more nuanced understanding of "value."

The average American earning $40,000 per year defines value as "getting the cheapest price." Most of us associate the word *value* with brands like Wal-Mart or the Dollar Store.

Affluent buyers think of value not in terms of the cheapest price, but in *return on their investment*. And when it comes to buying luxury homes, the "return" they are looking for is NOT financial. It is emotional. They want to feel good about their home. They want to be proud of it. They want others to be envious.

Not that the average American doesn't experience these desires—they just don't factor them into the home buying decisions. In a literal sense, they generally cannot afford to.

If you've studied psychology, you have probably heard of Abraham Maslow's "Hierarchy of Needs." Maslow theorized that there is a "pyramid" of needs. We can only attempt to satisfy the "higher" needs once we've already satisfied the "lower" needs. At the base of Maslow's pyramid are basic physiological needs (air, water, food, etc.) Once these basics are met, we then look for security. Once we've got *that* covered, we tend to pursue more abstract desires like social needs (friendships, family relationships, etc.)

At the top of Maslow's imaginary pyramid are spiritual desires like "achievement," "self-esteem," and "self-actualization." In a nutshell, once we have basic shelter and food on the table, we search for *meaning.* We want to be loved. We want to be appreciated.

In a very literal sense, buyers shopping in a lower price range cannot afford to worry about "fluffy" abstracts like self-esteem, achievement, or self-actualization (when it comes to buying a house.)

Affluent people can afford to pursue these desires with their real estate purchases. And they do.

Stop and think about it: is any home really worth a million dollars? Certainly the labor and materials are not. The sum of all the wood, concrete, flooring, walls, electric and plumbing, etc., typically doesn't even come close to a million dollars.

It's about *prestige*.

Paradoxically, the higher you move up the price pyramid the less price matters. Whether it's a year round house on the Chesapeake, an executive home with a golf course view in Bulle Rock, or a premium priced Canton condo on the waterfront, "value" is not a function of price.

From a purely marketing perspective, selling high-end homes is not about finding buyers.

It's about finding *a* buyer. Finding THE buyer.

In the Baltimore area there are many, many buyers out there for $200,000 homes. Because of how many qualified buyers there are shopping in this price range, this is probably the easiest price point at which to sell a home. The "days on market" statistic for homes in this price range is much lower than in any other price range. There is plenty of demand!

And it also means these homes have to be competitively priced and positioned—if comparables are selling for $190,000, you can't afford to overprice your listing at $208,000. It simply will not sell—there are too many alternatives for buyers to look at instead. There is competition in this price range!

On the contrary, when it comes to high-end *luxury* real estate, the basic rules of microeconomics do not apply. The "supply and demand" rules you were taught in high school are next to meaningless. Why? Because all of these economic principles make an assumption that is NOT true in the luxury market: rational consumers engaging in "perfect competition."

When economists dreamt up the idea of "supply and demand," they assumed people always made rational choices based purely on price. But, as we've stated, affluent buyers have an entirely different conception of value. They don't think of value as simply being "the cheapest price."

Price is merely *one of many* factors for affluent buyers. And, all things being equal, it's not a particularly important one.

Furthermore, there is little "competition" for luxury homes, on both the supply and demand sides. As far as demand goes, there is a relatively small amount of buyers out there with the bank account necessary to purchase a "luxury" home. And as far as supply is concerned, there are very few homes in Baltimore that would qualify as "high end." This creates an interesting market—the traditional rules of supply and demand simply do not apply like they do at lower price points.

Instead of science, it's art. Instead of mathematics, it's psychology.

And now that you understand the "why" of selling luxury homes, Paul will reveal the "how."

Without giving away too many of Paul's secrets, here are a few specific tips:

- High-end photography is a must (Paul also uses professional quality HD video). At lower price points, you can get away with taking your own pictures. The cameras on cellphones now are better than the digital cameras of just a few years ago—I see some real estate agents snapping property photos on their phones these days.

THIS IS UNACCEPTABLE ON A LUXURY LISTING. Hire a professional photographer to take the pictures. Yes, it will cost a lot more money. But if you are working with a real estate agent that refuses to invest a few hundred bucks into truly professional photos—on a listing that may generate a potential commission of $25,000—you should probably find a new agent! Oh, and make sure the photographer uses a wide-angle lens.

- When you write the property description, do NOT describe the features of the home. Instead, tell a story about the *benefits.* You may have heard the old advertising saying, "Sell the sizzle, not the steak." This is absolutely *crucial* when it comes to marketing luxury listings. Sell benefits, not features! Features are the desirable characteristics of a property—**benefits take it one step further and describe why the characteristics are desirable in the first place**, and specifically how the buyer's life will improve once they purchase the home. For example, DON'T say, "This wonderful home has a full size, in-ground swimming pool." Instead, say something like, "Imagine entertaining your friends on a hot summer day in your beautifully landscaped backyard—with an in-ground swimming pool! Instead of asking your neighbors if you can use *their* pool, be the family that other people have to ask! And if you have kids, they will love inviting their friends over for a day at the pool. *Your* pool, that is." Can you see the difference? Talk about the benefits (not the features) with effective storytelling. Create vivid images in people's minds of how much better their life would be if they lived in this home. With lesser-priced listings, you can get away with boring descriptions of the floor plan, the number of bedrooms, bathrooms, etc. Luxury listings demand more emotional, psychologically stimulating marketing.

- Create *targeted* buzz. Get some word-of-mouth going about your listing! This can be done in a multitude of ways. Without revealing all of my marketing secrets, here's a few ideas:

    o **Social Events.** Don't just hang out for 2 hours on a Saturday morning and hope people show up. Turn a luxury listing "open house" into a premiere social event that gets people talking! Have live music and expensive food (maybe hire a local chef or cater from an expensive, well-known restaurant). Yes, this will cost more money, but think in terms of value—not cost. Oh, and don't call it an "open house." You want as many people to attend as possible, not just the relatively few affluent buyers that are currently shopping for a new home. You want the public to think of the event as a fun evening to look forward to, NOT an open house. The more people that attend your "open house," the better. Word-of-mouth is the goal! And don't promote the event to the general public—you want the affluent social circles to think of your event as *exclusive*……because it is.

- **Creative Direct Mail.** Again, the purpose of sending out direct mail is NOT to find a buyer. Very rarely, if ever, will someone get a promotional letter in their mailbox….and decide to buy a million dollar home. Instead, the purpose of your mailer should be to drum up interest in the listing. Create some buzz! TELL A STORY about why the owners are selling, what a great opportunity it is, why the home is unique, etc. Don't focus on boring things like price, number of bedrooms, etc. The goal is to create an exciting mailer that peaks people's interest—EVEN IF THEY ARE NOT CURRENTLY LOOKING FOR A NEW HOME. You want them to tell their friends at coffee about that "interesting letter" they received in the mail. Remember, when it comes to marketing a high-end luxury listing, don't worry about finding buyers. Find

THE buyer. There *is* someone out there that is a perfect match. The job of a real estate agent is to do whatever it takes to generate positive buzz and word of mouth in the community so affluent buyers know about your listing......even if they aren't looking to buy a new home! All it takes is one person to mention it to a friend who IS looking.

- **Online Marketing**. These days it seems like EVERYONE is online. Especially on social media! Most agents upload their listings to the MLS, and maybe aggregate them on a few of the online directories like Zillow, Trulia, etc. Paul and his team take it one step further (well, a lot of steps further!) They **create an individual website for each listing.** That website will have a professionally filmed HD video tour, so potential buyers can "tour" the home from their couch. It will include a professionally written property description, and a way for interested buyers to contact him to find out more information. There is a certain amount of *prestige* when a property has its own unique website. And prestige is very important when it comes to high-end homes! Again, check out www.gteamsellshomes.com for an example. They also use Social Media to promote listings. They don't just post a link to the listing on Facebook—Paul actively promotes his listings with paid advertisements that his target market will see in their "newsfeed." Facebook has a very robust advertising platform that some agents completely ignore! It allows you to target very specific demographics of people. We can't think of a good reason why you would *not* use social media to promote your luxury listings.

**One last tip for owners of luxury homes:** do not try to "save money" by refusing to update the interior of your luxury listing.

This strategy can work with lesser-priced homes, but it almost guarantees that a luxury listing will NOT sell. Or, even worse, it will sell at a bargain, *lowball* price.

If you have outdated carpets, REPLACE THEM WITH NEW CARPET.

If your walls are adorned with early 1990's floral wallpaper, GET RID OF IT.

If your appliances were brand new when you moved in 1997, THEY ARE NOT NEW ANYMORE. Get new ones!

**Buyers of luxury homes will not tolerate anything that is outdated.** I mean, think about it: would you shell out a half million or more on a home that will immediately require $50,000 of upgrades? Heck no!

And again, the reason is not mathematical. It has nothing to do with price. Most affluent buyers that can afford a $500,000 home could just as easily afford a $550,000 home. So it's not the extra expense of replacing old, outdated appliances, carpet, fixtures, etc. It has to do with *convenience.*

Buyers don't want to worry about the stress and time involvement of managing an interior renovation. It's fun to watch on **HGTV**, but it's pretty stressful in real life.

If your home's carpets, appliances, countertops, fixtures, wallpaper, or paint colors are outdated, it's not their problem. It is *yours.*

Most affluent buyers are short on one thing: time. They may have flashy cars, take expensive vacations, dress in designer clothes, and have all the money in the world, but they have limited **time**. And trust us—they don't want to spend what little free time they *do* have shopping for carpets, wallpaper, or new appliances.

It has nothing to do with the money.

By definition, an affluent buyer can afford to buy all of these things, hire contractors to install them, etc. But that takes time! It's stressful. And if they have the option of buying a $500,000 home that immediately requires $50,000 of upgrades to make it "modern," or simply buying a similar $550,000 home that is newly updated and *move in ready*, guess which one they'll pick? They will choose the more expensive, contemporary home. Every single time.

In fact, **even if you discount the price of your home beyond what it will cost to make the necessary upgrades, it probably still won't sell**. Suppose you get multiple opinions and estimate that your home's outdated interior will need $50,000 of renovations. New stainless steel appliances, new carpet, new paint colors, stripping all the old wallpaper, new fixtures, etc. The whole nine yards!

If you don't want to deal with the nuisance of doing all this, remember: buyers won't want to, either. They'll simply pass on your home. Even if you discount the price by $75,000 (which is $25,000 more than the $50,000 of upgrades it requires), buyers will *still* avoid your house.

**Remember, when it comes to luxury listings……it's not math—it's psychology.**

And the higher priced the home, the more this dynamic

matters.

You can get away with this on a $200,000 home. At that price range, discounting the price by $10,000 to compensate can work. A buyer might think the outdated interior represents a bargain. In this price range, buyers don't really expect stainless steel appliances, granite countertops, fresh contemporary paint, or an updated bathroom. They'd much rather save $10,000 on the purchase price than pay more for a newly upgraded interior.

<u>This is not true of affluent buyers.</u>

Rather than dealing with the stress of worrying about a potential renovation, they'll simply look at homes that are *already upgraded.*

Affluent buyers don't want to mess around with wallpaper, paint, carpets and other projects *for the same reason you don't*! It's time consuming and stressful.

To be blunt: if you want your luxury home in Hunt Valley Country Club for example to sell for a good price in a reasonable amount of time, there cannot be outdated carpets, fixtures, bathrooms, kitchens, old wallpaper, or anything that may require "upgrading."

If you know that a particular part of your home is outdated, fix it BEFORE you list the home for sale. If you don't, it may be a long, long time before your listing sells.

    If ever.

# 6. The Fifteen Most Costly Mistakes Made By Homebuyers (And How To Avoid Them!)

### 1. Lack of Vision

As Mark Twain said, "You cannot depend on your eyes when your imagination is out of focus."

Ahhhhh—this is so true! It is almost shocking to me how most buyers have no vision. None. Nada. Zip.

Because of that, Paul absolutely *loves* working with buyers that have the rare gift of "vision." Most people simply don't have it.

When Paul first started in real estate over 5 years ago, he took this for granted! He just assumed his clients had the same "vision" he had for properties. You know, the ability to walk in to a disgusting, outdated, smelly, UGLY house……and instead see it for what it *could* be. What it *should* be.

Have you ever watched one of those reality TV shows about home renovations? "Property Brothers" on *HGTV* is one of our favorites. The basic idea of every episode is two brothers (one's a contractor, one's a Realtor) attempt to convince someone to buy a "fixer upper," and spend the difference on an extensive renovation budget.

For example, instead of buying a $200,000 house, you purchase an ugly, outdated home that needs lots of repairs for $140,000…….then spend the "extra" $60,000 renovating it into your absolute dream home.

Usually what happens is the buyer does not believe them. The property brothers try to convince the buyer that this *is* their dream home…..it just needs some work. The buyer is skeptical that a house "this ugly" could ever be modernized into a contemporary, updated home. In short, **they have no vision.**

Obviously, what happens is the "property brothers" and their crew renovate the ugly house into a BEAUTIFUL, updated home. Their vision allows them to see potential in ugly houses. And that's the big idea here. The key word is POTENTIAL.

Sure, there are plenty of properties out there that are just plain, butt ugly. There's no other way of saying it. And you know exactly what I'm talking about! Outdated carpets, kitchens, bathrooms, paint…..you name it. I've seen it all.

The Baltimore area has plenty of "outdated" homes. For the most part, all of the new construction (in the last 25 years or so) has been in the outlying counties such as Harford and Howard.

This means that for the "average" person who's looking to buy a $200,000 home in Baltimore County, **there are lots and lots of opportunities to find bargain properties.** Instead of buying a $200,000 home that's "move in ready," consider buying a $150,000 home that's cosmetically ugly and needs some repairs. Invest the difference in a custom renovation that will turn a bargain "fixer upper" into your contemporary dream home.

Remember: cosmetic problems are usually the easiest and most affordable fixes. Older kitchen cabinets, appliances, carpets, and paint are not terribly expensive to replace. In fact, you'd be shocked at how far $10,000 can go!

In many cases, you can *completely transform* a home with as little as $10,000 of cosmetic upgrades.

Using the above example of buying an ugly $150,000 property instead of a "move in ready" house that's $200,000......think of what you could do with a $50,000 renovation budget!

This gives you a massive advantage as a house hunter. It means you can research many more homes than the average buyer, because you aren't confining your search to the relatively few homes that are truly "move in ready."

**When you have vision, you have more options.** And when you have more options, you have leverage during negotiations. And that's a very, very good thing!

And, besides, being "move in ready" is pretty subjective. Everybody has different taste in interior design, layout, etc. Even on a home you originally think is perfect, you'll most likely change things.

Most of these ugly properties are usually passed by because buyers are so obsessed with homes that are "move in ready." As you know, homes that are really, truly, *move in ready* almost always have a premium price. This is especially true in the Baltimore County area, where most of the homes are at least 25 years old.

What this means for you is that if you have the patience and creativity to see the POTENTIAL in a home, you can score a major deal! Most buyers aren't willing to look at old, outdated homes. And if they are, they immediately want to move on to the next one!

It never even occurs to them that they could purchase an outdated/ugly home at a steep discount, and have plenty of money left over to completely renovate it into their dream home.

The vast, vast majority of house hunters only see the product that's there *right now*. They see the old carpets, the old paint, the outdated kitchen appliances, the poorly maintained yard. **People with vision see none of this; they see *opportunity*.**

## 2. Ignoring The *One Thing* You Cannot Change About A House

Rather than being concerned with cosmetics, here's the one thing you should *not* compromise on: location.

The old saying, "location, location, location" should be your top priority. It's a cliché for a reason!

Why? <u>Location is the one thing you can't change.</u>

This is a pretty profound insight: you can change ANYTHING about a house….*except location.* So when you find the perfect house in the perfect location, remember that anything and everything you don't like about it can be remedied!

Let us explain further….

Paul was working with a young couple, who we will call "Erin" and "Jon" (not their real names). They both came from upper middle class families. They were used to nice homes, newer cars, and all around being "comfy."

They wanted to buy their first house on their own, together. Their budget was *not* going to get them a newer house in an upscale neighborhood.

They needed to compromise.

Paul made some calls and set up tours at a few local properties with larger yards, which they had requested. Because they needed space and were on a lower budget, the homes that we viewed, well, tended to need a little imagination!

With some elbow grease, some rearranging of walls and a little money, some of these would have been close to perfect! The square footage was also what they were asking for.

But Erin and Jon lacked VISION.

They insisted on looking at houses that were "pretty," with very small yards and not much square footage. The house they chose *was* pretty. BUT....none of the homes around it were! They were "The Big Fish in the Little Pond."

**Erin and Jon broke one of the cardinal rules of real estate:** it's always better to own the worst house in a nice neighborhood than the nicest house in a bad neighborhood.

About a year later, when they were starting a family, they realized they already needed to move! To make matters worse, they took a loss on the house when they eventually sold it. Not good.

The previous owners had already made all the improvements, and, for the size, the house had met its maximum value for quite some time. Every home reaches a certain point where it doesn't matter how many upgrades it has—it simply cannot sell for more than X amount of dollars.

Against Paul's counsel, Erin and Jon bought a house that wasn't right for them. It's important for us to point out that the house they purchased wasn't intrinsically a bad house…..it was just a bad house *for them*. See the difference?

**Now, there is a happy ending to this story.** They DID listen the 2nd time around. They found probably the UGLIEST house ever. Seriously. It was *bad*.

BUT….the yard was perfect and the location was perfect for their job commutes. We went through the house with an open mind and came up with a renovation plan. We took down walls to open up the floor plan, added some nice fixtures, flooring, and really opened up the place. With some exterior renovating to put the icing on the cake, the house went from the ugly toad to the handsome prince!

About 3 years later, when Jon got a job transfer, they had

to sell. They were only sad until they held the check at their closing. They made over $50,000 profit!

LOCATION, LOCATION, LOCATION.

Oh, and a little vision doesn't hurt, either :) Keep an open mind!

## 3. Failure To Research and Interview *Multiple* Agents

You're probably thinking to yourself that you should pick the first agent that comes along. After all, we're all the same, right? WRONG!!!!

Imagine that you're out driving around on a Sunday afternoon looking at homes. You find a home that you really, really like. It's in the right neighborhood, and the yard has excellent curb appeal. Naturally, you want to find out more!

You decide to call the agent whose sign is in the yard. You meet with that agent, because you think they are the only one who can show you the house. WRONG.

Nowadays, most agents are part of the MLS (multiple listing system). That means that any of us can show almost any property out there.

So, BEFORE you call a total stranger whose phone number was on the sign, do a little research!

(One reason agents love "getting listings" is that yard signs generate lots of phone calls! The more yard signs they have, the more leads they get. We elaborate on this in the chapter titled, **What You Need To Know BEFORE Listing Your Home**)

Friends, we beg you: before making what will probably be the largest financial decision of your life, INTERVIEW SOME AGENTS!

Now, we're not saying you should automatically hire Paul. Don't get us wrong— we would both love to have the opportunity to work with you. Maybe we'd be a great fit! We sure hope so. But you should *always* do some research before hiring a real estate agent. It's a big decision!

We don't know of any businesses that hire the first person that applies for a job. Nope, that's not how it works. Usually the competition for job openings is fierce. The company's HR director will sort through dozens of resumes, and choose only a handful to actually come in for an interview. <u>Only then will they select the very best candidate.</u>

Don't you think you should put a little thought into who *you* hire?

ALWAYS, ALWAYS, ALWAYS ask for testimonials.

**Testimonials are the best kind of research you can do.** Take everything the agent says with a grain of salt. *Of course* they'll say good things about themselves. And that goes for us, too! Don't take our word for it; check out what our clients are saying about us!

Make sure the agent you pick knows the market. And we mean really, truly, *knows the market.* Real market wisdom takes years to hone. A rookie agent might be able to memorize "knowledge" by doing a few minutes of research on MLS statistics, but is this really *wisdom*?

Don't be someone else's learning curve!

- Are they local to Baltimore?

- How long have they lived in your area?

- Are they full time?

- Do they have advanced credentials? (There is a difference between *Realtors* and real estate agents in general. Being a certified *Realtor* is the difference between an accountant and a CPA, a business executive and an MBA, etc.)

- Do they come across as trustworthy?

- Are they able to answer your questions without hesitation?

Paul's team practices this principal of "knowing the local area" It is a disservice to the client if we do not know the area. For example, Paul currently lives in Bel Air. HE LOVES when he gets clients in Bel Air. However, he specializes in other areas as well. He has lived in and knows many areas of Baltimore. For example, Paul grew up in Arbutus and his family lives in Ellicott City. But if Paul had a client who was looking in say southern Anne Arundel county or Carroll County, Paul would hand that off to a member of his team the specializes in that area. The point is to ask how they know the local area.

## 4. Rushing Your Buying Decision "Because There's Other Offers"

Let me tell you about a "trick" some agents pull.....

Let's say you are out house hunting and you find one you really like. Naturally, you want to be able to check on some details before you write an offer. No one wants to rush into a buying decision on something as expensive as a home! Seriously—most people spend a few days doing online research of what *television* they're going to buy! With that in mind, you should NEVER make an impulse purchase when it comes to real estate. The stakes are simply too high. You're probably sitting there reading this thinking, "Well, duh! I knew that." All we can say is that you'd be surprised how many people get caught up in a whirlwind of emotions and make irrational decisions.

Think of how emotionally invested you can get when watching real estate TV shows like *House Hunters*.

You think to yourself, "NO! Don't buy *that* house. Are they stupid? Buy *this* one!" It's easy to get excited about buying a home, even when it's not yours.

That being said, if you've never experienced the thrill of shopping for a home, the emotions are exponentially higher when it's not some stranger on TV.

It's *your* home that will be paid for with *your* money. All of a sudden, emotions come into play! And, as is usually the case, savvy real estate agents understand the subconscious psychological forces that make otherwise smart people do dumb things.

Here's an example:

The agent gets pushy and tells you to hurry **because there's another offer coming in, and you don't want to miss out on this one!**

Let's be blunt: whenever we hear that "there's another offer coming in," we're immediately skeptical.

When you hear the sellers tell you to *hurry and make an offer*, all sorts of things should be running through your mind...

"What's the condition of the roof?"

"I wonder if there's hidden mold damage?"

"I really genuinely do like this house, but I feel rushed."

Many buyers will hear this and their emotions get the best of them—they make a rushed decision and place an offer. This ploy works because the human brain is wired to fear loss more than it desires gain. Psychologically, it's more traumatic to lose something we already have than to not gain something we never had in the first place. You might be thinking "Sorry fellas, that doesn't make any sense. You never owned the home, so you weren't really losing it!"

Sort of.

When a showing goes well and buyers really like a home, they start to picture themselves in it. They visualize it being their home. They really truly do think it is their home! So when they hear the seller's agent say, "Hurry and make an offer, there is another buyer interested," alarm bells start to go off in their heads.

It would be emotionally traumatic to lose out on their dream home (never mind the fact that there's probably ten other homes out there that could be their "dream home").

The problem is that every once in a while, there actually *is* another offer on the table. Unfortunately, it's a perfect example of the boy who cried wolf. How can you really know?

Our advice in situations like this is to ask yourself, **If this home was priced $20,000 higher than it currently is, would I still want it?**

This question is a good litmus test on whether or not the home is truly perfect for you. If it is really your *dream home*, you will be willing to spend the extra money to make sure it's yours. If not, keep looking. There will be other homes you "fall in love with." Trust us.

Most people are not willing to slightly "overpay" for a home unless they are 100% convinced, beyond a shadow of a doubt, that this is their DREAM HOME. In that case, buyers will do pretty much anything to win the bidding war.

So the next time you hear, "Hurry and write an offer, there are other offers on the table," remember to ask yourself: would I be willing to pay an extra $20,000 for this home?

If not, keep looking!

Trust us on this one......people make decisions emotionally, and then attempt to justify those decisions with logic. This is one reason it's so important to have a trustworthy agent that sees when you are getting prematurely "excited" about a property, and can bring you back down to Earth.

It may be okay to make an emotionally impulsive decision on what to have for dinner, but it's probably not a good idea on a $150,000 (or more) purchase!!!

Let's get back to the story :-)

2 weeks later, you find out that there really was no other interest and it's a ploy that agent uses to get his listings sold. Ugh. You move on and find another property. You LOVE this one!

Not learning from your first mistake, you call the agent on the sign.

After touring the home, your emotions are escalating. This home has all of your must-haves! It's got an open concept floor plan, spacious backyard, and the kitchen is newly updated. You decide this is *the one.*

Again, this agent says you will need to make an offer within the next 24 hours because "there is already one serious offer on the table."

Thinking that you won't be outsmarted this time, you call their bluff. *Except they're not bluffing.* There actually was a serious offer, and you lose out on this one!

You scramble, trying to offer more than asking price, throwing in every possible incentive to get that seller to take your offer. TOO LATE! Contracts are legal and binding. The seller had to keep the original offer.

Lesson learned.

## 5. Losing Money By Ignoring The Power Of Negotiation

*In business as in life, you don't get what you deserve, you get what you negotiate.*

–Chester Karrass

Earlier, we touched on *location, location, location.*

Well, there's another word you need to commit to memory: *negotiate, negotiate, negotiate!*

To avoid leaving money on the table, you'll need an experienced agent who understands the "art" of negotiation. For the most part, the skill of negotiating is something that is developed through experience. Like most things in life, the more you do it, the better you will get.

And that brings up an important question: **how are you supposed to develop the skill of negotiation when you will probably only buy/sell a few homes in your lifetime?**

The answer is simple: you need to trust the experience of your real estate agent.

We have participated in hundreds of negotiations. From mortgages to homes, we have represented both sides of the table: buyers *and* sellers. When you consider how many deals we've been involved with, doesn't it make sense to rely on the experience of your agent and loan officer?

In fact, this is how free enterprise works! In a free country, everyone gets really good at one specific thing. Economists call this process "specialization" or the "division of labor."

The entire point of a free economy is that people

specialize in something, and then rely on other people to do what they're *not* experts at. This is why I'm more than happy to pay plumbers, auto mechanics, and accountants to do their respective jobs—we sure as heck wouldn't be able to figure it out! And it's why they rely on *us* when it comes to buying and selling real estate.

It *pays* to use experts. It doesn't cost you anything.

And here's why an expert negotiator can save you so much money (or make you money, depending on how you look at it): there is no other activity, on a per hour basis, which can generate the returns of good negotiating.

If you think doctors or lawyers make good money, consider this: they usually make a few hundred bucks an hour. Let's say $200. At the rate of $200/hour, it would take 25 hours to generate $5,000 (before taxes and all of that stuff.) So a lawyer has to work 25 hours to earn $5,000, assuming they are billing $200/hour.

For the average middle class family in the Baltimore area buying a $300,000 home, you could "earn" $6,000 in two hours of negotiations. **That's $3,000 per hour.**

Whoa.

If you're buying a home, and you negotiate that the seller

pays all closing costs (commission, home inspection, bank fees, etc.), that can *easily* add up to $8,500.

Maybe you can get them to lower their price by $2,500 and agree to cover $6,000 of your closing costs…….you just earned $8,500! EVERYTHING is negotiable. The appliances, artwork, furniture, closing costs, home inspection, moving expenses, you name it. It all depends on your creativity.

Keep an open mind, and find a win-win solution!

You should know that the more expensive the home, the easier it is to "make money" during negotiations. On higher priced luxury homes, it's not uncommon for people to negotiate in $25,000 increments.

"I'll give you $650k."

"Nope, I need $715,000."

"Well, how about $675k?"

"Could you do $690,000?"

When you really stop and think about it, this is *crazy!* The average American earns around $30,000 per year, and in many real estate deals that much money can be made or lost in a split second decision. And it all depends on how skilled you are at negotiating.

For the average person, there is no easier way to earn money than developing solid negotiation skills. Period.

And if you aren't the type of person that feels "comfortable" negotiating, this is yet another reason why it's so important to work with a real estate agent you *trust*.

In many situations, a real estate agent can save you more money during negotiations than you actually pay them in the commission fee. So it actually costs you money to *not* work with a professional agent!

Paul's going to share a quick story to illustrate what we mean:

*I met a really nice couple. We will call them Nancy and Ryan. They wanted me to do a market analysis on a house they had just purchased 12 months prior in Abingdon. When my market analysis report came in $10,000 under what they had paid less than a year ago, <u>they were shocked.</u>*

*I have NO idea how that financing went through, but it did.*

*The agent they had at the time said it was a steal and convinced them to write a full price offer "before someone else snapped it up."*

*I later found out that this agent had the listing for 5 1/2 months and was about to lose it to another agent when her listing contract expired. Needless to say, she wanted to sell it quickly. Not very ethical, but it is what it is. And the kids believed her.*

*There was NO negotiating at all. None.*

*After trying for weeks to convince them that they needed to lower the price, they still wouldn't budge. Reluctantly, I let them list it for "their" price. Of course, there was no interest, no showings, and no offers. 2 months later, they lost the house across town they wanted because theirs didn't sell.*

If you buy/sell a few homes over the course of your lifetime, it's not unrealistic to say that you could earn (or lose) $100,000 based on how skilled of a negotiator you are. Think about how that will affect your retirement lifestyle, your kids' college savings, or the amount you can donate to your church!

Moral of the story? Learn how to make money at the negotiating table!

**PS**

If your agent is knowledgeable, he or she will also tell you when you SHOULD write that full price offer. There *are* times that it's actually necessary. If a property truly is a high demand property (maybe in foreclosure, an estate sale, or other special circumstances), it could be priced to sell quickly.

Occasionally, those properties *do* get multiple offers on them. You may be coached to offer more than the asking price. This can happen! Again, we can't stress enough the importance of having the right person giving you advice.

As we've stated like fifty times in this book, it's all about TRUST. You've gotta *trust* your agent! If you don't.....find a new agent!

## 6. Being Intimidated By "The Numbers" (And How To Make Over $100,000 In 20 Years Or Less By Buying Instead of Renting)

Don't be blinded by numbers!

What do we mean by that? Instead of seeing the big price tag, think about *affordable monthly payments*.

Remember: if you buy a house for $180,000 in Dundalk,

you aren't expected to write one big check for $180k. Nope—you make monthly payments! So instead of obsessing about the final sales price, think about the "price" of your monthly payments. Can you afford them? If so, don't let the *big number* intimidate you.

And, really, this is truly a miracle from a historical perspective. For centuries, the average person lived in total poverty. Without our modern financial system that allows people to make affordable monthly payments, hardly anyone would be a homeowner. That's why many people define homeownership as **the American dream.**

Think about it: even for a "starter" home priced at $175,000, how long would it take you to save up the entire $175,000?

You could probably do it, but it would take years……probably *decades*. Is it worth it to you to wait *decades* to invest in a home? Probably not.

If you're 30 years old right now, you might be sixty before you finally have saved up enough money to buy a house. That's a pretty big price to pay!

Without getting too philosophical here, the one thing you can't get more of is *time.* Everything else in life can be replaced: cars, clothes, jobs, computers, etc. But even the richest man on Earth cannot buy himself another year if he is dying. Time is not unlimited. It's a finite resource. It's the one thing you can't buy more of.

You can't exchange dollars for more time………*or can you?*

When you agree to finance a home purchase by paying for it with a "mortgage," you are essentially trading dollars for time.

You are agreeing to pay a little bit more (what we call "interest") for the privilege of owning a home NOW, instead of having to wait until you've saved up enough money to write a check for the entire amount. And that could be *decades* away….

For many folks, they will never have enough money saved up to buy a house. For example, if you're making $50,000/year, you will probably never be able to save up $100,000 to buy a house. After all of your living expenses are factored in (taxes, insurance, gas, food, etc), there's simply not a lot of money leftover every month. It would be extremely difficult, if not downright impossible, to save up $100,000 to buy a house without a mortgage.

That's why mortgages are so amazing! It allows the average American to invest in homeownership by making monthly payments. Most people would agree that they'd rather pay some interest on their monthly payments to actually *own* a home, rather than renting for years and years and years.

Oh, and did we mention that when you rent, there is an "opportunity cost" to that money?

Let's say it takes you twenty years to save up $200,000 to buy a house. This means that you're saving about ten thousand dollars a year, or $832 per month. **After 20 years of saving $832 per month**, you finally have enough money in your savings account to go out and buy a $200,000 house!

But look at the *opportunity cost* of the situation……instead of saving that $832 every month in a savings account (which pays little to no interest) how else could you have invested that money?

Imagine that when you started saving your $832/month you were 25 years old. This means that you'd be 45 by the time you're able to buy your house! And you won't be living in a high-end luxury home……$200,000 will buy you an average, middle class American home.

**In Harford County you can buy a solid starter home for $180,000**, but in most other areas of the country that same home could cost you $250,000 or even $300,000. So we're using very conservative numbers here!

With a budget of $200,000, you won't have high-end appliances, newer flooring, an updated kitchen, modern bathrooms, a big yard, or any of that stuff. So keep that in mind....

Here's the **opportunity cost** of the situation: during the twenty years you were saving up $832/month, you needed to live somewhere. You probably rented. Let's say you were spending $1200 on rent (most people spend more than that!).

You've probably thought about this before, but it's worth repeating: renting is like flushing money down the toilet!

When you pay rent to the landlord (fancy term for whoever owns the home), you are essentially paying his bills, his mortgage, his expenses, etc.

<u>But you never see that money again.</u> It's not like when you move out you can ask for all the rent money you've paid. If you pay $1200/month in rent, as soon as you mail that check, it's *gone*. Forever.

This might scare you: for the 20 years you've been saving up money to buy a house, **you will spend about $288,000 on monthly rent!!!!!!!!**

Don't believe me? 20 years is 240 months. 240 months times $1200/month equals $288000.

Yikes!

So if you think paying interest is so terrible that you're willing to wait 20 years to save up enough money to pay cash……are you prepared to live in your parents' basement that entire time? If not, be prepared to spend $288,000 on rent money!

Moral of the story? Clearly, it makes sense to focus on the *monthly payment.* NOT the actual sales price.

Yes, you will pay more than the "sticker" price once interest is factored in. And yes, some financial gurus like Dave Ramsey think it's a terrible idea to pay interest on a home (for the record, we *love* Dave Ramsey and most of his advice is spot on).

But once you factor in the opportunity cost of paying all of that rent money, the decision is easy: go buy a house!

Whenever you hear someone say that homeownership is "too expensive," train yourself to ask the question, *expensive relative to what…..renting?*

**ESPECIALLY in the Baltimore area, this is a no brainer!**

Look at the rent costs in Towson or Columbia. Heck, even White Marsh. It is expensive.

In Baltimore, homes are cheap enough that renting makes ZERO sense. We know it's a pretty bold statement, but think about it: if you have the financial discipline and responsibility necessary to own a home, why would you pay rent money?

<u>When you pay rent, it's basically a 100% interest payment.</u> You are not paying any principal. You are not building any equity. Once that money is spent, it is gone.

This is not the case in all areas of the country. In some cities it actually makes financial sense to rent, because homes are so expensive (places like San Francisco, New York City, etc.) In that case, there would actually be an opportunity cost of *not* renting. This is NOT true about Baltimore and her suburbs, homes are very affordable here! That's why people who work in D.C. are willing to live in Baltimore. You can get a lot more for your money.

If you're paying $1,200/month in rent, why not invest *that same amount of money* every month in a mortgage payment? In a very literal sense, it wouldn't cost you a single penny to become a homeowner (there *are* programs out there to buy a home with ZERO DOWN.)

Sure, there will be costs associated with homeownership that don't exist for renters. Renters don't have to pay to re-shingle a roof every 25 years, upgrade aging furnaces, or redo the siding. But renters *are* paying for these things, indirectly. The rent money they pay every month gives the homeowner the cash to make these improvements.

Wouldn't you rather be the one *receiving* money than sending it?

When you pay your own monthly mortgage, you're basically *paying yourself.*

After interest is deducted, the money you pay every month pays down the balance of your mortgage. It's really no different from depositing that money in a savings account every month!

Think about it: if you're renting for $1200 it equates to $14,400 per year. Wouldn't you rather have that $14,400 in *your* "savings account" than the landlord's?

By buying instead of renting, you are spending the same amount of money—but instead of that cash going to the landlord it's being deposited into your home equity "savings account."

Eventually, you'll pay the mortgage off entirely and there

won't be any more payments!

The $288,000 you would have paid is now cash in your pocket—the money you would have spent on renting all those years.

## Seriously! What would you do with an extra $288,000?!!

Unless you plan on moving out of the area in the foreseeable future, there is really no reason to rent.

We would say that the average Baltimore couple can expect to pay about $1,500/month in rent. **Wouldn't that same $1,500 a month be better spent on a mortgage payment? $1,500 a month can buy you a lot of house in certain areas!**

Yes, there will be other expenses. Property taxes, home maintenance, etc. But keep in mind that when you are renting, you are indirectly paying for all of these things anyways. Where do you think the landlord gets the money to pay for all of these expenses—*you*!

Now, you probably think we're biased because of what we do for a living. That's probably true…..but you cannot ignore the simple math.

Would you rather pay $1,500 every month in rent, or

make a mortgage payment on your own property? One path guarantees you will live your entire life month to month, just trying to scrape by with enough money to pay the bills. One path leads you to financial freedom. Which one will *you* choose?

It's a no brainer!

So if you're looking for a house and you put a certain dollar amount in your head as the "maximum" amount you are willing to spend, you could be missing out on some great opportunities! Many buyers, even before checking with their loan officer, decide what they want to spend. They let the "big number" get in the way.

Why? **Because it intimidates them.** They get scared. They can't conceptualize paying that much money for something—it just *feels* like a big number.

For instance, they will think about a $250,000 house and only see that big dollar amount. To make matters worse, they will figure out how much interest they will pay on that amount, over the next 30 years.

It seems like a logical thing to think about......and 30 years seems like a ridiculously long ways away!

Instead of stressing about the big number, focus on the affordable monthly payments. Are you comfortable with *that* number? If so, buy the house!

With today's interest rates being incredibly low (which could change by the time you're reading this book), you would be surprised at how low the payments really are.

Let's say you've decided that you don't want to spend a dime more than $250,000. But a house comes along that's listed at $269,500. It is absolutely *perfect*. It's your dream home. Your real estate agent tells you that you can probably get it for $260,000. *But that's $10,000 over your limit.* You don't have an extra $10,000 laying around!

**Instead of looking at the sales price, focus on the monthly payment.** Especially when interest rates are reasonable, the difference in monthly payment between a $250,000 and $260,000 mortgage is………..about $50 a month.

Can you handle an extra $50/month to live in your dream home? For most of us, the answer is YES!

Don't let a fear of big numbers intimidate you! Focus on a monthly payment that you can comfortably afford.

## 7. Having Unrealistic Expectations With A Smaller Budget

Let us tell you about some first time homebuyers we worked with....

"David" and "Emily" (not their real names) wanted to look at homes in a certain area. When Tom ran the numbers he came to the conclusion that they would be on a tight budget. Keep in mind it was their very first home, so they weren't spending $350,000. Well, they weren't spending even *close* to that.

To be honest, they weren't even spending *half* of that.

But they were used to spacious, luxurious homes (both came from somewhat wealthy families), so they had **completely unrealistic expectations.** They were assuming they could buy $300,000 worth of house for a little over $200,000. Paul knew from the start this would be an interesting house hunting process!

David and Emily needed a reality check. Paul took them out for coffee at The Sunny Day Cafe in Bel Air and tried to explain this to them. They didn't really listen to him when he tried to tell them that their wish list of "must haves" was completely unrealistic for their budget.

And we mean COMPLETELY UNREALISTIC.

They wanted four bedrooms, newer hardwood floors, an updated kitchen, a modern master bath suite, and yard "suitable for entertaining."

Paul had to muster all of his professional courtesy to not to spit out his coffee when they handed him their list of "must haves." He actually thought for a moment that he might be the victim of a reality TV show prank. No way they were actually serious! It would be hard to find a home that satisfied their list even with a budget 50% higher!

They were off in fantasyland, to put it nicely.

That first meeting at the Sunny Day Cafe didn't go very smoothly. They claimed to "understand" Paul's concerns, but tried to convince him that if he looked hard enough, he would find the perfect home that Tom would be able to get financed for them.

*Sorry folks, Paul and Tom may be entertaining at times but they are no magicians!*

We can help you find a "stretch" home that might be a

little bit out of your price range (and maybe convince the seller to sell it at a price you can afford), but we can't magically double your budget. Tom can help you find the mortgage that best fits your needs but he doesn't control interest rates and programs.

We're not the federal government. We can't just print money!

Anyway, they must have looked at 20 homes! They were absolutely *determined* to live in the same area as some of their friends, but honestly, there was nothing in their price range that even came close to *remotely* satisfying their wish list.

The homes that *were* in their price range needed extensive repairs—repairs that would require money David and Emily did not have.

Paul FINALLY convinced them to look in a neighboring town. They ended up purchasing a beautiful home, at a price well under their budget……**that was nicer than what any of their friends had.**

As we've stated before: buy the neighborhood, not the house.

And keep an open mind.

This is more important than ever when you're buying

your first home, and you're used to living in somewhat nicer housing. We get this a lot with young people in their 20's. Even the college dorms today are pretty nice, so many of these first time homebuyers have a completely unrealistic expectation of what a "starter home" is all about.

**If you're 20-something years old and reading this, pay attention!**

The entire concept of a starter home is pretty self-explanatory: it's a home for you to "start" your home ownership experience. It won't be luxurious. It probably won't be spacious. It won't have a newly updated kitchen or a beautiful bathroom like you see in the home and decorating magazines. A starter home is usually small (two or three bedrooms), and has one bathroom. Sometimes two.

In the Baltimore area (and surrounding communities) we would classify anything around $200,000 or less as a starter home.

A starter home will allow you to build a solid credit history, because the monthly payments will be extremely affordable. **Especially in Harford County!** Houses here are incredibly affordable relative to renting.

As we've stated elsewhere in this book, this is NOT TRUE

IN OTHER AREAS OF THE COUNTRY. In fact, usually when one of us has to go out of the area (or out of state) to industry conferences, our colleagues are absolutely **shocked** when we tell them how affordable homes are in our market.

The usual reply we get is, "Why would ANYONE rent? If homes are that cheap, everyone should buy!"

We can't argue with them.

And truth be told, it's a great feeling knowing that you have money left over every month. Many people make the mistake of buying exactly what they can "afford," so there's basically zero dollars leftover every month for entertainment, vacations, etc. Trust me—this will really stress you out!

It's better to buy an affordable starter home that's well *beneath* your budget, and have plenty of "breathing room" every month. You'll be a happier person, we guarantee it. As your career develops and you start earning more money, *then* you can look into buying a nicer home with a larger mortgage payment.

Do NOT buy a "reach" home (where you're reaching a bit beyond what you can actually afford) as your first home. This is a HUGE mistake.

Remember: a starter home is all about building a solid

financial foundation.

A starter home will not *only* help you build a solid credit history. It's a great learning experience! Owning a home gives you an entirely new perspective on "living." When you own the house you live in, you will notice things you didn't notice before.

- The condition of the siding.

- The condition of the shingles on the roof.

- The efficiency of your "HVAC" systems.

We could probably rattle off a dozen more, but here's what we're getting at: home owners have to be responsible for many things that tenants take for granted. This awareness gives you a new perspective on the true cost of having a brand new kitchen, updated bathroom, new flooring, etc.

**Homeownership is a crash course in the value of a hard earned dollar.**

Tenants will often complain that the kitchen is ugly, the bathroom needs to be updated, or the carpets need replacing. When you become a homeowner, you realize how expensive this stuff is, and all of a sudden it makes sense to you why most landlords don't spend gobs of money updating their properties—it simply doesn't make financial sense!

Doing a minor kitchen renovation could set you back $10,000. Updating a bathroom can easily cost a few grand! New flooring adds up quickly, too. For a landlord to justify investing this much money back into a house, he or she would need to charge a lot more in rent..........which *very few* renters are willing to pay.

Once you own your own home, all of these things start to make sense.

Instead of having vague thoughts in your head like "I deserve a new kitchen," you start to count the cost. It teaches you the value of a dollar! And it psychologically prepares you to buy a "nicer" home in the future *by understanding what you're paying for.*

Owning a home will make you a more responsible person, period. It teaches you to look at things from a value perspective instead of an entitlement perspective. And that's a good thing!

With any luck, your home will appreciate while you own it. So not only will you build up equity by paying down the mortgage every month, you will increase your net worth through appreciation of your home's value (there are ways to "force" appreciation that we cover elsewhere in the book.)

In summary, investing in a "starter" home is a very, very valuable thing to do. It will allow you to build your credit, become a more responsible person, and financially position you to invest in your "dream home" someday.

A journey of a thousand miles begins with a single step....

So don't let unrealistic expectations stop you from buying your first starter home!

## 8. Not Conducting A PROFESSIONAL Home Inspection

No kidding, we could probably write an entire book on the subject of home inspections. So it may be hard for us to stay focused and narrow this down to a few pages! *That's how important it is to have a home inspection.*

Seriously.

Long ago, home inspections weren't really that common. Sometimes a buyer would have a trusted friend take a look at the house (usually an electrician, plumber, or someone they knew with construction experience). It wasn't anything formal, and it didn't really affect the buying process one way or another.

Homes were bought and sold like a 4th grader trades his baseball cards.

Professional investors were much more likely to do their "due diligence" on a property, because they needed to know the deferred maintenance, future renovation expenses, etc.

But for the average residential homebuyer, **you basically had to trust that the seller wasn't hiding any problems.** And for many homes, that was quite a leap of faith.

Today, it's pretty much standard to have a professional home inspection before closing on a house.

If you don't already know, a home inspection involves a home inspector going through everything in the house and making sure there are no problems. The only thing a home inspector cannot do is check out what's inside the walls. Home inspectors will check the roof to see the condition of the shingles, they will check the siding, they will examine the walls and ceilings for signs of water leaks, they will check all sinks/faucets, they will check the power outlets, they will check the age/condition of the HVAC system components, etc. It's a very thorough investigation!

On an average size house, a home inspection will take approximately 3 hours.

Typically it costs $300 or $400 to have a professional home inspection.

The buyer pays for the inspection.

**Trust us on this one—it will be the best $400 you ever spend.** We've had instances where a problem was discovered during the routine home inspection that potentially saved the buyer over ten thousand dollars. That's a pretty good ROI!

<u>We think you're crazy if you buy a home without getting a home inspection!</u>

You can breathe a sigh of relief once the home inspection report has been filed! The only thing a home inspector *can't* do is rip open the walls to see what's inside, or start tearing open the flooring. Other than that, the home inspection should reveal any potential problems, fixes, and repairs that need to be made before closing.

**Following a home inspection, it's pretty common for a buyer to request that the seller make a few repairs prior to closing** (problems that were discovered in the home inspection).

<u>But let us be very, very, very clear on this:</u> the home inspection is not meant to create a "laundry list" of repairs for the seller. Unless you're moving into a brand new home, there *will be* maintenance issues, things that need repair, etc. It's just

a fact of life.

A good home inspector will coach you through all of this, and teach you how to be proactive when it comes to "preventative maintenance." Your car regularly needs oil changes, tire rotations, etc.—so does your house! If you fell in love with a great used car, you wouldn't *not* buy it because it's in need of an oil change. The same goes for purchasing a house....don't let minor, correctable problems get between you and your dream home!

If the extent of the repairs is over a few hundred dollars, you may need to renegotiate the price if the seller isn't willing to make those repairs. Again, consult with your real estate agent and home inspector. It's ultimately up to you, but they will be able to provide you with the wisdom necessary to make the right decision.

And remember: everything is negotiable.

Paul will almost *always* advise his buyer clients to include an "inspection clause" in their offer, **meaning that their offer is contingent upon a successful home inspection.**

This allows you to walk away from a deal—even *after* you've made an official legal offer—if the inspection reveals the home isn't up to your standards.

And the beauty of this clause is that "your standards" are legally subjective. What this means is that you can say the house "failed" the inspection…..*for any reason.* You can literally point to ANYTHING in the home inspection report and use it as an "escape clause" from a potentially bad deal.

**And assuming the seller accepts your offer with the contingency included, this is completely ethical.**

There is nothing shady about using the home inspection clause to exit a deal. If the home inspector finds something that you feel is a deal breaker…..*then it's a deal breaker!* This can be anything from a leak under the bathroom sink to a few missing shingles.

But, keep in mind, if you truly want the house, you won't allow a few minor repairs to stop you from buying the house.

In fact, we would venture to say that it's nearly impossible for a home inspection to *not* reveal things that need to be repaired.

It is almost guaranteed that the home inspector will discover problems with the home. When you hire a home inspector, you should EXPECT there to be problems detailed in the report. Usually, these problems are not a big deal.

AND THIS IS WHERE MANY HOMEBUYERS FREAK OUT.

**Pay close attention here:** because of potential liability, a home inspector is incentivized to make things sound worse than they probably are.

Consequently, many homebuyers freak out when they receive the home inspection: "Oh my God! There are 4 missing shingles, the kitchen sink leaks, and one of the windows needs to be replaced!"

At this point, you need to *slowwwwwwww down*.

Try to evaluate the situation logically and not emotionally. Replacing a few shingles, fixing a basic leak, and replacing a window is *not a big deal*.

In fact, most everything short of finding dead bodies hidden in the basement can be fixed.

Do NOT let the home inspection intimidate you or scare you. Know that the home inspection report will make it sound much worse than it actually is (the home inspector doesn't want to get sued, so he will exaggerate problems and write down every single defect he can possibly find).

Now, don't misunderstand our point—we're not saying you should ignore the home inspection report. We are saying that you should look at the big picture.

Don't let a few imperfections scare you away. You will end up spending money on "maintenance" anyways……it's better to proactively find out then *react* to a problem that has compounded over time!

Can you think about the "band-aids" you have used to cover up little leaks, stains, or broken items? Paul (of course) has a pretty good story about that….

*"It was actually the very first house I sold. My client was so excited to be purchasing her first home. She was an older lady who worked really hard to get where she was in life. This was a very exciting time for her. It was also an exciting time for me. This was my first sale after all. All the stars were aligning! Then, it was home inspection day. On the disclosures it stated that the basement leaked occasionally. My buyer was not overly concerned. The inspector discovered some moisture on the block wall in the basement. My client still being excited decided to move forward with the transaction. The day after settlement I got a call that her basement was full of water. I am not telling you this to scare you. I am telling you this so you know to put stock into what the inspection report has to say. Also, if the sellers had not disclosed that the basement leaked occasionally then they would have been in big trouble."*

If it is ever proved that you knew about something and

did NOT disclose it, you are in deep legal trouble.

Of course, the best thing to do is make the repairs.

**Here's what you need to remember:** always, always, always have a home inspection before buying a house. Just don't let the home inspection report scare you away from investing in the home of your dreams!

## 9. Letting Friends, Family, And Other Non-Experts (That Generally Don't Know What They're Talking About) Influence *YOUR* Decision

We'll try to keep this section short and sweet!

Do NOT allow unsolicited opinions from friends, family, or other non-experts to have too much influence on your home buying decision.

(The exception would obviously be if you have friends or family that work professionally in the real estate industry)

We've heard this too many times to count…..

***"Paul, our parents need to look with us!"***

### *"T.J., my cousin used to write mortgages"*

If your parents will be living there with you or your cousin will be signing the mortgage with you, fine. No judgment.

If not, do some independent research on what YOU want, go house hunting, find your top 3 houses, THEN bring them in to look……….after you've already toured the properties yourself.

We *completely understand* that you trust your parents' wisdom and experience. After all, they've probably bought/sold multiple homes, so they probably can provide some helpful long-term perspective. But that doesn't mean you abdicate all responsibility and decision making to them. Don't let them override you!

We see this all the time: a young couple falls in love with a home. It's in their budget and it's in the right neighborhood. But the parents don't like it for some reason. Not wanting to insult their parents, the buyers walk away from a deal. After all, **they don't want to ask for their parents' advice and then ignore it.**

But keep in mind that *your parents are not real estate experts.*

If there is something inherently wrong with a deal, the

real estate agent will advise you accordingly! If you like a home, the real estate agent thinks it's a good fit, and the bank agrees to finance the mortgage……..do it! At that point, any other opinions are exactly that—*opinions.*

You wouldn't let your parents perform brain surgery on you just because they are your parents. The same goes for your friends, co-workers, or anyone else that feels the need to tell you what you should or shouldn't buy.

**Politely thank them for their suggestions, and then do whatever you were going to do.**

We are *not* trying to disrespect parents. We both have children. We will help our children buy their first house. Luckily, we do this for a living. We know the market. We will let them do the initial research, and narrow it down to just 3 homes. From there, we would ask some detailed questions but ultimately, *it will be their decision*.

This is where it's most important to find professionals you TRUST. This is a constant theme throughout the book: finding an agent and loan officer you *trust*.

As a parent, if you see the top 3 homes your child selected…….and you hate them all…..talk to the agent!

Part of the problem may be price range. Don't worry if

your son or daughter can't afford their dream home at age 25!

It's far better for them to build a solid credit history, learn the ropes of homeownership, and become a financially responsible young adult than it is to buy a "stretch" home at the top of their budget that leaves them broke at the end of every month because of an expensive mortgage payment.

The other issue we sometimes see with well-intentioned parents is comparing the current market to what it was when *they* purchased.

We can't tell you how many times we have heard, "Well when we bought our house in 1970, it was only $40,000 and it was twice this size!"

Ummmmm............inflation. Most everything was "cheaper" in 1970 because the dollar was worth more. That doesn't mean your son or daughter is getting ripped off buying their home. If it's priced well *relative to the market right now*, that's all you need to worry about!

Advice is good, but *don't make unrealistic comparisons.* You will be frustrated, and so will everyone else.

## 10. Expecting The Home buying Process To Be As Fun

## As It's Portrayed To Be On *HGTV* (The REAL LIFE Process Of House Hunting Is Way More Confusing, Stressful, and Difficult Than It Looks On Television.......Why You Shouldn't Let This Intimidate You)

In the next few pages, we're going to reveal a secret about how hit TV shows like "House Hunters" are set up behind the scenes.

.........You didn't *actually* think it was real, did you?

But first, some honest advice about house hunting.

The home buying process doesn't always go smoothly. And especially if it's your first time buying a home, the process can be downright *scary*.

Let's be brutally honest here: it's intimidating.

There are lots of forms to sign. Lots of paperwork. Lots of meetings.

It will seem like T.J. wants all sorts of things from you: recent paycheck stubs, last year's taxes, bank statements, a credit report, DNA samples, first born child, etc.

**You WILL get stressed out. Accept this as a fact before**

**you get started.**

All sorts of things will be running through your mind....

*Title insurance…..wait, what's a title? And what am I insuring?*

*And I heard something in the newspaper about a property tax levy. How do I register to pay property taxes? And I don't even know what a levy is. Doesn't it have something to do with rivers and dams? After all, there are many rivers and dams in the area! But I guess I'm not sure. Which reminds me, should I get flood insurance? Is that even a problem in Baltimore? Hmmmmmm……..*

*Speaking of insurance, I need to insure my home! Where do I go for that? Does it cover fire damage? Hail? What if we have a water leak? And how much does it cost?*

*Cost…..yikes….I wonder what utilities will cost every month. Will someone send me a bill? Or do I have to go somewhere to pay it?*

*And who will pay the mortgage every month? Do I have to drive to the bank every 4 weeks? Can I set that up on auto-pay?*

*I also remember something about a deed. I have no idea*

*what that is. Does that cost extra? And closing costs.....how much will those be? And what exactly am I paying for? What is closing, anyways? Is something open that needs to be shut?*

As you can see, if you've never bought a home before, the process can be confusing!

Here's our advice to you: accept the fact that at some point, you WILL be overwhelmed. You WILL be stressed out. You WILL be confused. You WILL be afraid to ask a "dumb question." You WILL start to experience doubts. You WILL question whether or not buying a home was such a good idea.

This is completely normal. *Everyone* experiences this.

Trust us on this one: it's much easier to navigate the home buying process when you are mentally prepared.

If you acknowledge ahead of time that there will be things you don't understand, you won't let it dominate your thoughts.

Real life is not like HGTV.

**Here's an insider secret about how most of these real estate reality TV shows actually work: it's all staged!**

With the popular show *House Hunters*, the couple has already purchased the home they end up "selecting" in the end.

Sorry if we just ruined the fun for you (I feel like I'm telling a young child that Santa Claus isn't real!)

On shows like *House Hunters*, they are basically pretending the entire time that they are looking at homes. In reality, they've already chosen the home they are going to live in. They've already bought it!

The show is usually filmed after the fact, and then they go out "house hunting" and pretend that they haven't actually decided. One of the homes they tour is, in fact, already theirs.

It would be like watching the *Bachelor* knowing that prior to filming, the bachelor was already married to the show's "winner." It's all a pre-planned show.

To put it bluntly, it is fake.

This is because in the real world, it's not all sunshine and rainbows.

Most couples on *House Hunters* look at 3 homes and, magically, find their dream home. Every single time. Seriously, does anyone believe that this is legit?

House hunting is more complex than the 30 minutes of edited footage you see on TV.

There might be bumps in the road. Actually, let me

rephrase that. There WILL BE BUMPS IN THE ROAD. In fact, there might be some 12 inch potholes deep enough to get lost in.

Figuratively, not literally.

Whether it's a home inspection issue, a financing issue, or just not finding what you're looking for, be *patient*! Remember your goal.

You don't want to be a renter any longer. You want to be a home OWNER. The financial security that comes with owning your own home, and the *feeling* of owning your home……..will make everything worth it.

Trust us!

## 11. Not Signing A Contract With A Buyer Agent

I'll get straight to the point: do NOT simply call the phone number on the yard sign.

Why? The phone number on the yard sign is the listing agent's phone number. The listing agent is contractually obligated to represent the best interests of the seller. Not you.

This means that they won't really give you objective information, advice, or insights on the property. They have one goal and one goal only: sell the house for as much money as possible. After all, that's what the seller wants!

The listing agent doesn't care if the home isn't right for you, or if you can't afford it. They don't want to hear your excuses……they just want you to buy it!

<u>The listing agent is a salesman, pure and simple.</u>

Think about it: as a buyer, does it make any sense, whatsoever, to work with someone who is legally obligated to do what's best for the *seller*?

Instead, find an agent you TRUST. Find an agent you are comfortable with. And then sign an exclusive contract to work with them!

What this means is that they are obligated to do what is best for *you*. They will research homes for *you*. They will submit offers for *you*. They will negotiate for *you*. They will do what's in your best interest, not the seller's. This is a huge advantage!

**And the best part?** The buyer's agent only gets paid when you actually buy a house (usually their commission is paid *by the seller*).

So you can rest assured that you are getting objective information from your buyer agent. They have no incentive to lie, mislead, deceive, or try to convince you to buy a home that's not right for you.

YOU are their customer. Not the seller. They want to do what's right for *you*. If they don't, they won't get paid!

Unfortunately, many buyers simply do a few hours of online research, drive around and look at some properties, then call the number on the sign. Many times they will talk with 5 different agents in a month!

Guess what? Most agents really aren't interested in working with you if you aren't "loyal" to them. This isn't because they feel entitled—it's just not a good use of their time to spend hours and hours with someone that might end up buying a home with another agent. It would be like a car salesman spending lots of time with a customer, taking them on multiple test drives, helping them understand the financing, and then……..the customer buys the car through another salesman.

Clearly, real estate agents don't want to invest a bunch of time and money into a client that views the various agents as interchangeable commodities.

When you sign a buyer agreement contract to work exclusively with one agent, that agent is now incentivized to work for *you*. They will have *your* best interests in mind.

And remember: **they don't get paid until you actually buy a new home!**

In fact, we can't think of a good reason why you would *not* work with a buyer agent!

Of course, it's important to make sure you choose the agent that's right for you. I've said it 100x in this book, but it's vitally important that you *trust* your agent. That's what it ultimately boils down to. When you trust that your agent will do what is right for you, it takes a lot of stress out of the home buying process!

To see some of our marketing strategies or to custom search for homes visit **www.gteamsellshomes.com**

## 12. Ignoring Your Home's Monthly Income Potential (Monthly Cash That Could Be Used For Your Car Payment, Savings Account, Or Helping You Qualify To Buy A Larger House)

Your home doesn't need to *cost* you money every month.

In many situations, you can live for free. Or even make a *profit* every month by owning a home.

No, we're not referring to some pie-in-the-sky scam that will leave you broke and penniless. This is a proven, real world strategy. The results speak for themselves.

This strategy is used by hundreds of people in the Baltimore area. Many of them are our clients, and many of the homeowners using this little known strategy are personal friends.

In fact, **T.J. used this strategy with his first house** to generate some extra income.

Do you want in on the secret?

Here it is: renovate part of your home into an apartment

to generate rental income.

**It's that simple.** All you need is a separate entrance, a kitchen, bathroom, and bedroom(s). In many homes, *the basement is perfect for this.*

Perhaps an inspirational story from a client will help....

## *They laughed at me for wanting a home that was "out of my price range." Until I bought it.*

My friends and relatives thought I was crazy. Naïve. Maybe a little stupid.

But I went ahead anyways and bought a home in a really nice neighborhood. A neighborhood and a home *far* out of my price range.

How did I do it?

I'll reveal that at the end of this story.

I was 27 years old at the time, and I just didn't feel like waiting until age 40 to buy my dream home. Life is short, and I didn't want to postpone my dreams.

When you stop and think about it, time is the most valuable resource we have. Money is important, but you can always earn more of it. Time, on the other hand, cannot be bought. No matter how wealthy you are, you cannot petition the gods to add years to your life. You may be able to afford world-class healthcare that will keep you alive a bit longer, but when your time comes, your time comes.

That being said, why do so many of us tolerate living in "starter" homes for five years, ten years, fifteen years?

Don't get me wrong, I'm all about financial responsibility. I have savings accounts, investment accounts, and a 401K.

I am not saying you should just "seize the day" and buy something you totally can't afford. Don't allow fluffy, positive psychology to lead you into bankruptcy! That's not courageous. That's just stupid.

If you use your imagination, you'll quickly discover that you *can* afford many things you previously thought were unattainable.

Here's how I did it: Tom (T.J.) Barker told me I was approved for and could comfortably afford a $250,000 mortgage. In Baltimore $250,000 will buy you a pretty good house, far beyond the "starter" category of minimalistic 2 bedroom townhomes.

But....there was a problem. I wanted more house than $250,000 would buy me. I wanted my dream home......*now.* So, I put my brain to work and started thinking.

Tom gave me some advice that I still remember to this day: "If you really want something, don't ask yourself whether or not you can afford it. Ask yourself *how* you can afford it." This changed my life.

I gave my Real Estate agent instructions on where I wanted to live and what I was looking for in a house and what I was willing to pay for it. She proceeded to tell me I was being un-realistic, but I would not be deterred. I knew what I wanted. *(I just love clients like this! – Paul)*

Then one day I got a call from my Agent. She had found a home with potential. I was nervous when I heard the work "potential." It was in my desired neighborhood and it was in good shape. The interior was a little dated but that wasn't a big deal.

There were two problems:
1) It was listed for $50,000 above my desired sales price
1) It didn't have a finished basement

But Tom's advice made me think: *how* can I afford this home?

My agent felt that we could negotiate the price of the home down to approximately $280,000 because the couple who owned the house was eager to sell. The difference between my comfortable payment and my dream home payment was less than $450 per month. I was determined to make it work, somehow.

All of a sudden I realized that by converting the unfinished basement into a rental apartment, I could earn $600 per month……money that could be used to offset the cost of my mortgage! Yeah, it would take a little money to convert the basement, but I didn't let that stop me.

I had a buddy who worked as a general contractor come over and take a look at the basement to give me an idea of how much it would cost to fix up the basement.

He told me that it was going to cost around $25,000.

That hurt.

I already was going to have to come up with a down payment of 20% and closing costs. Luckily my grandparents were willing to help me with some of the down payment. Now I had to figure out how to pay for the work to be done to the basement.

I put my team to work. My agent was able to negotiate an additional $10,000 from the sellers to go toward the closing costs. Tom qualified me for a program that only required a 5% down payment vs. the traditional 20% down payment. Yes my payments were a little higher than I hoped but the additional rental income still covered the difference.

Thanks to reduction of the down payment and the help from the seller, I was able to have the work done to the basement and had someone renting it within 90 days of settlement.

Now not only can I comfortably afford my dream home but I am able to pay a little extra to the mortgage every month.

One more thing—I will probably be earning a lot more money within 5 years as I advance in my career. As I earn more and more, the "risk" of this deal decreases proportionately.  In the near future I won't have to rent the basement out.

Sometimes it's fun to prove people wrong ☺

With a little creativity and a good group of advisors, I was able to buy my dream home more than a decade before most of my friends.

To be totally honest, I think my neighbors expected me to sell the place within the first year. Not because they were mean spirited, but because they didn't see how I could possibly afford the house! After all, I was a young guy that bought a big home in a nice neighborhood.

This property was supposedly out of my league. Except that……it wasn't.

I want to emphasize again that I didn't simply buy a house way out of my price range, and cross my fingers hoping I would have the money each month to make the mortgage payment.

There is a difference between stupidity and ingenuity! Avoid the former, but embrace the latter.

I used my creativity to develop *a plan*. It wasn't about luck. I did research and made a plan, and then followed through with it.

Following Tom's advice, I asked myself *how* I could afford it, not *if* I could afford it.

The moral of this story is simple: think outside the box. Don't let someone else's idea of "financial responsibility" limit your lifestyle.

**-Josh R. – Timonium, MD**

## 13. Giving Up Too Easily (And Underestimating The Power Of Creativity)

We're sure you've heard the expression, "Where there's a will, there's a way!"

This cliché is 100% true when it comes to real estate.

Because the average person is not buying or selling

multiple homes every single month, they don't realize how flexible terms can actually be. We see it happen far too often where "conventional" financing won't work, and a buyer gets discouraged and quits. Sometimes they feel embarrassed that their credit score isn't perfect. They feel shame in not being able to qualify for a "traditional" mortgage with a bank, so they simply walk away.

They give up.

This is a big, big mistake.

What's going on in situations like this is the buyer believes that, "Everybody else qualifies for conventional financing! I must be a loser if the bank won't loan me money."

They get discouraged, and embarrassment prevents them from exploring creative options. Buyers don't want to be perceived as *desperate*, and they certainly don't want to experience "failure" again.

**Newsflash**: many, many, many people don't qualify for traditional financing.

Either their credit score isn't good enough, they don't have enough money saved up for a down payment, their expenses are too high, their income is too low, etc.

Usually, you actually have enough money to make the monthly payment, but your "ratios" aren't up to the bank's standards. For example, banks usually don't want you to be spending more than 30% of your monthly income on a mortgage. So, hypothetically, if you're earning $1,000/month, the bank won't lend you money to buy a home if the monthly mortgage will exceed $300—which is 30% of your income. There are other metrics the bank will look at, but the point we're trying to make is that often times you actually do have the money to make the payment every month, but you're not as financially stable as the bank would like you to be. The bank doesn't want to risk having you get behind on your payments (or going into default,) so they refuse to make the loan in the first place.

This wasn't always the case—when the housing boom was in in full swing a few years ago, many banks weren't even doing basic credit or income verification. Anyone, and we mean anyone, qualified to buy a house. Even with nothing down! It was crazy. This was because the local banks would "originate" the loan, then larger government-backed institutions would "buy" the mortgage from the local bank. At that point, the local bank that created the loan didn't have any risk. The mortgage wasn't on their books. If the homeowner defaulted, it wasn't their problem. This obviously created a conflict of interest, because the people profiting off of loan origination didn't really have any incentive to do basic due diligence on their borrowers.

If you were a buyer, this was great! You didn't need to worry about qualifying for a mortgage……*everyone* qualified. Today, this is not the case. And it's why we're writing this chapter, to reveal some lesser-known alternatives to financing your home purchase.

Remember: the bank only loans money to people who don't need it!

Let's go back to the common cliché I mentioned earlier…..*where there's a will, there's a way!* Creative financing techniques can work if the buyer is motivated AND the seller is motivated.

In fact, **if the seller is motivated**, pretty much anything is possible. Sometimes the seller just needs to get rid of a house, and they will do anything necessary to make the deal "work." As a buyer, this is a perfect situation to be in!

Maybe they owe money for something else, and the only way they can come up with the cash is selling the house.

Maybe it's an estate sale, and the family just wants to sell the property and not have to worry about maintenance, taxes, etc.

Maybe the seller is moving out of state for a new job, and needs to sell quickly.

Maybe the seller is a landlord and is sick of managing tenants.

Whatever the motivation, the first step in creative financing is working with a motivated seller. If the seller isn't motivated, none of the creative strategies we will teach you will work—the home will most likely be purchased by another buyer who *is* qualified for normal financing. From the seller's perspective, it's easier to work with a buyer who's prequalified for a mortgage. They get a lump sum check from the bank, and that's that. It's far more convenient for the bank to finance a property.

But, like we said, if a seller is desperate--and they're running out of options--they *will* be open to more creative alternatives.

**The first step is making sure the seller is motivated!**

If the seller is motivated, nine times out of ten the most common financing strategy involves some form of "seller financing." This means that instead of using a bank as the "middleman," the buyer will make payments directly to the seller. Sometimes this is called a "contract for deed." Instead of paying the bank a monthly mortgage payment, you pay the money directly to the seller. There is no bank involved.

Typically, the seller will charge a premium to compensate for the risk and inconvenience of not using a bank. Usually, homes sold on a "contract for deed" will have the interest rate be a few points higher than a traditional mortgage. So, if a conventional mortgage is 6%, the seller may demand 8%. The specific numbers will obviously vary depending on the market.

Sometimes, the seller will demand a small down payment, sometimes not. Usually, they will want at least a little bit of money down, to make sure you (the buyer) have some skin in the game. Often, the down payment will be much less than the traditional 20% down that banks require. Sometimes, the seller will request 5% down, or 10% down. But not always—if the seller is motivated, you *can* find properties for zero down. I'm not saying you *should* do this, but it is possible.

If there's a will, there's a way.

Phrased differently: if the seller is motivated, a deal can and will happen.

Sometimes a seller isn't willing to finance the property forever, but they will for a year or two. They are hoping you will qualify for a "traditional" mortgage in that time frame.

Sometimes the seller will be open to "bartering" for services. If you're an auto mechanic, perhaps you can trade services as a bargaining piece. Would the seller value free oil changes for five years, along with free car maintenance? The only way to find out is to ask!

The worst that can happen is they say "no."

"Creative" financing options aren't for everyone. Sometimes it can be a really bad idea. Other times, it's exactly what is needed to make a deal happen that otherwise wouldn't.

And this is yet another reason why it's so important to work with a real estate agent that you *trust*. A good real estate agent can guide you through this process and make sure you are aware of the various options. They will make sure you understand the risks, the pros and cons, and what is ultimately best for *you*.

Every situation is different!

If you really want a specific house, and the seller is motivated to sell it, your creativity *can* be a wonderful substitute for money. Just because a bank won't loan you money doesn't mean someone else won't. Don't give up!

Where there's a will……there's a way.

## 14. Buying "Too Much House," And Then Stressing Out Every Month Over How In The Heck You're Going To Make the Mortgage Payment

Elsewhere in this book, we try to convince you that often you *can* afford more than you think you can.

This is because it pains us to see buyers say "no" to a home that they love, because it's $10,000 (or whatever) over their *arbitrary* budget. When it's amortized over a 30-year mortgage, the difference in monthly payment just isn't that much money.

However, the opposite is also true. **And probably worse.**

Buying a home that is too expensive for your budget virtually *guarantees* you won't be happy. Even if you love the home!

Think about it: is it better to err on the side of buying a home that's maybe too small for your family (and having extra money left over each month), or buying a home that's out of your price range and having to constantly worry about paying the mortgage?

A monthly mortgage payment is exactly that: it's a ***monthly*** payment.

If you struggle to make the payment in April, it's going to be just as hard to make the payment in May. And June. And July. And so on.....for the next 30 years (or whatever the term is for your mortgage.)

Unless your finances change for the better (you get promoted, get a higher paying job elsewhere, inherit money, work weekends on a hobby business like wedding photography, etc.) a monthly payment that stretches your budget will continue to stretch your budget.

Is it worth it?

I'm not even going to pretend that the answer to this question is subjective. It's not a matter of opinion. Trust us on this one—it's simply NOT worth it.

If you don't have a specific plan that details how you will pay for a home that is "out of your price range," then you have no business even *looking* at these homes.

Every dollar you pay in a mortgage payment is a dollar you cannot invest for profit somewhere else.

*At best*, the "equity" in your home resembles a savings

account. It's really not an "investment" in the same way a mutual fund, stock, or bond is.

We're not saying real estate is a bad investment—We're saying **the home you personally live in** should not be viewed as an investment.

Even worse, it should not be your *only* investment.

Your home is not a magical ATM machine. Don't assume it will constantly increase in value, allowing you to borrow against it with home equity loans.

Don't put all your eggs in one basket!

For many Americans, their home is their only "investment." They have no money invested in stocks, bonds, mutual funds, CD's, land, rental real estate, actual businesses, precious metals, or other investment vehicles. If your home equity reflects your net worth, you're in trouble if the local housing market dips—even temporarily.

If your home appreciates in value and your equity increases, then great. Think of that as a *bonus.* It's icing on the cake. Don't attempt to rationalize a mortgage payment you can't afford by convincing yourself that the home is an investment.

**That mentality got *a lot* of people in trouble a few years**

**ago...**

Paul was one of them.

"Even though it's incredibly embarrassing, I want to tell you my personal story. Hopefully, you can learn from my mistakes....

In 2007 I purchased a home in Harford County. I had a choice between a non-garage town home and a garage one. I said to myself... Well, you know if you buy the one without the garage you will regret it. You know it is an investment and the value will increase. I'm sure my income will increase. Aww hell let's get the bigger one even though it is a stretch.

We had a severe decline in income for a period of time. We rented the basement out to our friend Andy to subsidize the mortgage. It worked for the time being. However, many, many thousands of dollars later, we still own that home and rent it out. It took everything I had in me to get it to a cash neutral position. Note the year in which I bought it. Of course since it was the nicest town home in the community so its value has dropped the most since the real estate decline. The bottom line is, make sure it is the right home for you or it could take a long time to recover."

Patience IS a virtue. Step back, take a reality check, and

buy with your pocket book…….not your heart.

If you buy a home with a mortgage payment so high (and remember, "high" is completely relative to your specific individual income and budget) that you don't have any money left over every month for savings/investment accounts/vacation fund/emergency fund/entertainment money………you will be miserable.

Let me repeat that: **you will be miserable.** Regardless of how nice your house is.

(Trust me….I was *miserable.* – Paul)

It's simply no fun to have to turn down your friends when they ask you if you want to go shopping next weekend at Towson Town Center, go get crabs and a Natty Boh at Bo Brooks', or go to an Orioles game.

Do you *really* want that extra bedroom, or high-end updated kitchen, if it means you'll only have $20 per month of disposable "entertainment" income? Or zero?

Who cares if you have a nice home in a nice neighborhood if you can't enjoy life?

There is a difference between buying a "reach" house that is slightly out of your price range (with a specific plan on how you will pay for it,) and buying a home that you simply cannot afford *with no plan whatsoever of how you'll come up with the money every single month.*

And let us repeat that for emphasis: **every single month.**

In fact, some months it will actually be worse than others!

**For those of us living in Maryland, our housing expenses fluctuate with the seasons.** Your utility bills can be *much* more expensive in the summer due to cooling costs that simply don't exist in the winter.

So if you're stretched so thin that you're worried about making the monthly payments, things will only get worse come summer time. Factor that in when you're putting together budgets and figuring out "how much house" you can afford!

And remember: it is not worth it to have a monthly mortgage payment looming over your head every month that you can't afford.

It is stressful.

You will *not* enjoy living in a larger, newer home if you never have extra money to buy new clothes, go shopping, go out to eat, take vacations, etc. You will end up focusing on what you can't have instead of what you do have. And that's no way to live!

It's much, much, much, much better to invest in a home you can comfortably afford, and have extra money left over each paycheck to "have fun" with. And that's assuming you're financially responsible and have already allocated some money to retirement savings, the kids' college fund, etc.

Don't worry—as your career develops, you *will* earn more money and someday be in the financial position to buy the "dream" house you've always wanted.

If you've always dreamed of an $800,000 home on the Chesapeake Bay, it can happen! With diligent saving, a successful career, and responsible financial decisions, of course. Just don't buy an $800,000 home when you're making $50,000 per year—even if you can somehow "justify" it.

<u>In fact, that's a pretty good rule of thumb:</u> if you have to attempt to justify why you can afford a house……..you cannot afford it.

If buying a home requires clever rationalization on your part, it's better to use that mental energy to earn more income and make smarter investments…….so that someday you *can* buy that $800,000 Chesapeake waterfront home. And not think twice about the price tag.

Don't let your emotions get the best of you—you will be happier with a home you can actually afford. Trust us.

## 15. Not Getting Pre-Qualified For A Mortgage

We can't think of a single good reason why you would NOT want to be prequalified for a mortgage. It makes the house hunting process so much easier!

In one of our ads promoting this book, we stated that after reading the book, you would know the "number one mistake made by homebuyers."

Well, this is it.

**The number one mistake made by homebuyers is NOT getting prequalified for a mortgage.**

When you get prequalified, everything else falls into place. You know exactly how much you can spend, so you don't waste time looking at homes you can't afford (online or in person.) This will make *your* life less stressful, *and* your real estate agent's job easier.

Getting pre-qualified is the most important step to house

hunting!

There's nothing more disheartening than to fall in love with a house.....only to find out that you can't afford it. It's even more humiliating when you place an offer "contingent" on financing.....and the financing falls through.

To get prequalified, the first step is finding a loan officer that you can TRUST. And it might not be at "your" bank.

Just like finding the right real estate agent, finding the right loan officer is really important! They are not all the same. It's worth your time to "shop around" and figure out which loan officer best fits your personality, needs, etc.

Sometimes you will really like your bank, but you don't "click" with the loan officer there. Sometimes the opposite happens—you don't really like a particular bank, but you enjoy working with a loan officer that works there. My advice would be to go with whatever loan officer you are most comfortable with.

*(If anyone needs a recommendation for a Loan Officer, I know a REALLY good one! – T.J.)*

It should be someone you can actually look at face to face—beware of online financing! There are a few companies out there that are probably reputable and trustworthy, but there are many scams out there as well.

They are not ALL bad, but why risk it?

We can virtually guarantee that you will be much happier (and less stressed) if you work with a local bank that has a *physical presence* in your community. You're in luck, because it's our belief there are more mortgage companies per square mile in Baltimore than any other city in the country. We have both national and locally owned "regional" banks as well as direct mortgage lenders, so you will have options when it comes to financing!

It's really nice to know that if you need to speak with your Mortgage professional that you be face to face with them in less than 30 minutes if need be. You can't do that when your mortgage is handled by an online finance company.

There's just something to be said about good old fashioned face-to-face conversation!

Unlike books, movie tickets, or other items commonly purchased online, a mortgage is difficult to process in the virtual world. It's simply too complex and personal of a process to be handled well online.

Maybe that will change in the coming years—We're sure people were originally skeptical about many things that are sold online today. But right now (we're writing this book in 2014,) Paul advises his clients to avoid online mortgages.

It's simply too risky!

We have both seen deals fall apart the day of closing and have also seen "good deals" be everything BUT good. Unscrupulous Loan Officers have a way of sneaking in some last minute "surprise" closing costs. This is how they remain profitable even though their advertised mortgage rates *seem* like really good deals (usually better than the rates at local banks.)

For example, instead of the $6500 you were "quoted," you get to the closing table and find out they have some extra fees tacked on…..and your closing costs are really closer to $8000!

It's usually a much better idea to "keep it local," and work with a local lender that is truly part of the community.

Local lenders have accountability and incentive to serve you and get the deal done in a timely manner—it's much easier to complain about bad service when it's a local company than it is with an unknown online company.

**Local banks can't afford to have negative word of mouth circulate in a community, so they are usually dedicated**

**to providing great service!**

You get what you pay for.

# 7. Dos and Don'ts for Choosing The Real Estate Agent That's Right For *You*

Buying a home is one of the most complex and expensive purchases you will ever make....and it's not a purchase we would recommend making on your own!

Unless you have direct experience in the real estate industry (maybe as a property investor, mortgage broker, lender, home inspector, etc.), it will be extremely hard to "wing it."

And even if you have experience in real estate, you are still putting yourself at an *extreme* disadvantage by not being represented by a licensed agent (preferably a certified Realtor.)

To avoid making expensive (potentially *very* expensive) mistakes: you have to understand our local market, know where the inventory is, what the short term and long term trends are, how to negotiate, what contracts and inspections to perform, how to effectively market your listing or efficiently search for your new home.....the time you have to invest can cause you to pull out your hair if you don't know what you're doing!

Trust us on this one—84% of "for sale by owners" eventually list their home with a licensed real estate agent. Why? Because eventually, they figure out it's a lot harder than it looks. Specifically, a lot more time consuming!

There is a reason we hire real estate agents. But whom should you choose? What should you look for in an agent? It's not an easy choice, but here are five things you *shouldn't* do and five things you *should* do.

### 1. ***Don't*** **choose the first agent you meet**

Let us ask you a question: would you marry the first person you met? Of course you wouldn't. The same logic applies when it comes to choosing a real estate agent ... even if the agent is a referral!

While it's not a long-term commitment like a marriage, buying or selling a home is a huge, high-stress endeavor (if you don't believe me, ask anyone who has bought or sold real estate). You want to make sure you've picked the *right* person to help you navigate those waters. And that person might not be me!

We're not writing this book to convince you that Paul Gillespie *is awesome and all the other agents are terrible.* Instead, we hope this book is a valuable resource that empowers you to ask the right questions and make a more informed decision

**Here's the bottom line:** we have some amazing, highly professional agents here in the Baltimore area. Our goal is to help you pick the agent that is right for *you.*

Get as many recommendations as you can, and take the time to interview several real estate agents. Ask each agent questions like these:

- Are you a member of the National Association of Realtors?
- Will you show me houses listed by other realty companies?
- How familiar are you with the area?
- How long have you been in real estate full time?
- What is your average list price/sales price ratio?
- What is the average DOM (days on market) of your listings?
- Can you provide a list of testimonials? Will they have contact info on them if I wanted to reach out and validate them?
- What is your strategy/plan to help me find a home?
- Do you work weekdays and weekends?
- What makes you an expert on local real estate?
- Why should I choose you over other agents?

Compare the answers with your other interviews, and choose an agent who best matches your personality, style, goals, etc.

It's sad, but most people do more research on what car they want to drive than what real estate agent they work with. While car shopping, they'll do research online, physically go to a few dealerships, take a few test drives, compare and contrast, *then* they make a decision.

Very few people do this when it comes to buying/selling homes. They just call the number on a yard sign, or take a blind recommendation from a friend without doing any "due diligence."

Trust us—you'll be much happier with your buying/selling experience if you are happy with the agent you chose. Do some research!

## 2. *Don't* hire someone just because he or she says what you want to hear

You want an agent who will challenge you. Who will tell you when you are wrong. Who will keep you from making a huge (potentially six figure) mistake. Many agents are so concerned with not offending their clients that they are afraid to be blunt with them. To me, this is really, really important.

**If one of us were a buying or selling, we would want an agent that was absolutely *brutally honest* with us.**

We don't really care if a retail associate at Target or Best Buy sugarcoats a product, or tells us what we want to hear to massage our egos. If one of us ends up making a dumb decision on a $50 item, it's not really a big deal. Even something more expensive like a TV is fine. Life goes on….*but when it comes to the biggest investment (and debt) of your life, you want to know exactly what you're getting into*!

Agents that are not brutally honest are doing you a HUGE disservice. They are afraid the client will get mad and fire them. Paul would rather you fire him because he gave you honest advice (that may have temporarily offended you) than watch you make a stupid mistake that costs you a lot of money…..and then proceed to tell the whole town "how bad of an agent Paul is." Word-of-mouth travels quickly. Especially in the age of social media like Facebook!

We can't afford to let my clients make expensive, preventable mistakes. And they *definitely* can't afford it!

Look for someone who is assertive but not obnoxious. Ask him or her how they would respond if you wanted to make an offer on a house they knew was way beyond your budget, make a lowball offer in the wrong situation, or any other ethically difficult situation.

Long story short: a good agent does what is right for *your* wallet, not theirs.

### 3. *Do* Work with a Buyer Agent

Did you know that all real estate agents are deemed to be working for the seller *unless* there is a written agreement that says otherwise?

That's why a "Buyer Representation Agreement" is a smart move for anyone in the market to buy a home. There really aren't any exceptions to this....it is ALWAYS in your best interest to work with a buyer agent that is representing *you*—not the seller.

Buyer's agents come in a few flavors:

**General Buyer Agent**: Many real estate brokerages have designated buyer agents that primarily work with buyers. These agents usually don't have a lot of listings, so the potential for conflict of interest is a bit lower. Any agent or broker, however, can enter into a *Buyer Representation Agreement* with you to help you find a home and protect your interests.

**Accredited Buyer's Representative**: The ABR designation signals that an agent has taken advanced courses specific to buyer representation, and along with meeting other requirements has been accredited for working specifically with homebuyers.

**Exclusive Buyer Agent**: Exclusive buyer's agents never work for sellers, because they don't take listings and neither does the brokerage they work for. Instead, these agents work *exclusively* for buyers.

This is the only form of buyer agency that completely eliminates a conflict of interest between your agent/broker and the seller.

If you're working with anyone other than an exclusive buyer agent, the possibility exists that you will want to buy a listing that is held by the agent you're working with or the brokerage firm that agent works for. This is a situation called **dual agency**, and it means that the seller has already received the bulk of the guidance from the brokerage, but your representation might become more "neutral."

Now, let's be very clear. We don't want you to misunderstand what we are saying here: *there is absolutely nothing illegal or unethical about dual agency.*

The only potential problem is that a real estate brokerage is put in a situation where it has to balance loyalties between both parties, which can lead to some sticky negotiating situations.

Typically a real estate agent working on a "dual agency" transaction will lower their commission, slightly *(I'm actually not allowed to publish commission rates—contact an agent for specific details – Paul.)*

Again, this is not required by law, but you should know that it's pretty standard practice.

The buyer's rep agreement doesn't have to be in writing, but it does show that the process and commitment have been thoroughly explained. You CAN ask for representation and receive it *even if you aren't willing to sign the contract.* But don't expect that an agent will remember you or what you need……which may allow a more committed buyer to get YOUR dream home!

Make sure there is an escape clause in your contract so that you don't get trapped into a shady long-term agreement with an agent you dislike. Paul always allows his Clients the utmost flexibility when it comes to working with him. He wants to ensure that he truly is the right agent for the client.

## 4. *Don't* hire agents who don't know how to negotiate

As you certainly know by now, the real estate industry (everywhere, not just Baltimore) is full of part time, inexperienced real estate agents. These are the last people you want to help you buy your new home (and a good reason why you should choose a member of the *National Association of Realtors*).

But even for those who have made it a full-time career – and thoroughly enjoy what they do – if they are afraid of conflict and don't have sharp negotiation skills, they are not going to maximize your experience. And by that we mean "dollars" ☺

Look for a real estate agent who's not afraid to make tough requests or knows how to deal with a lowball offer.

## 5. *Don't* hire agents with abnormally high transaction numbers

Every market has real estate *superstars*—agents that have figured out how to leverage their time and money so that they can generate hundreds of thousands of dollars (sometimes millions) in annual commissions.

*Do not hire them.*

That might sound counter intuitive…..wouldn't a successful agent have a better chance of being successful with you considering their wonderful track record?

Well, no, not really. You see, a successful agent may or may not have what you are looking for. You and that agent may define success very differently.

One agent may define success by the number of transactions he closes a month, the amount of commission he makes, the number of awards he's accumulated.

Another agent might define success with the number of healthy relationships she's built, satisfied clients she has, or the number of video testimonials she receives.

One agent is all about himself. The other is all about you. Choose the one who is in alignment with your personality and goals.

Again, we're not saying "successful" real estate agents are to be avoided altogether. If they have high transaction numbers, *clearly they know what they are doing.* But you need to know what you're getting into! You don't want to be an anonymous "number" in their sales statistics.

And to achieve high "production" numbers (industry insiders use the word *production* to signify how much commission dollars they've "produced",) it's almost impossible to dedicate yourself to each and every client.

If an agent is all about **their** goals, it's hard for them to focus on **yours**.

Find an agent committed to *you.*

## 6. *Do* choose an agent who deals with homes in your price range

To most non-experts, selling a home seems pretty straightforward ... no matter if the home costs $50,000 or $5,000,000. Truth is, you should choose an agent who is an expert in your price range.

Just as doctors specialize, so should real estate agents. Price ranges will vary from market to market, but in the Baltimore area you could probably break them down into:

- Under $250,000

- Over $250,000 but under $500,000

- $500,000+ (We devoted an entire chapter to the topic of high-end "luxury" homes)

You should also look for agents familiar with the style of home you want to purchase:

- Condo

- Second home

- Luxury

- Relocation

And, obviously, choose an agent who is an expert in the area you want to live. For example, we wouldn't use an agent from Westminster to sell a home in Glen Burnie. Even if she is your best friend and is a rock star agent in her respective town.

If you're unfamiliar with the area, you will not be an effective agent. Period. This principle scales down, too. If you are familiar with Parkville but don't know anything about the neighborhoods around Arbutus, you will not be a very good agent for someone wanting to buy or sell in Arbutus. The fact that you are knowledgeable on Parkville neighborhoods is irrelevant in this situation.

If you are interviewing agents, ask them if they are familiar with the specific neighborhood/area of town you plan on buying or selling in.

## 7. *Do* pick an agent who matches your personality needs

Good real estate agents approach the art of buying and selling houses differently because they know that each client is different in personality and needs. Some agents even specialize in dealing with particular client types.

In her New York Times article Who's Got Your Back?, Vivian S. Toy identifies four such real estate agents:

- **Hand-Holder** – This person will be slow to speak, slow to make a move, and will be patient when you have a thousand questions to answer. This person won't mind answering the same questions ten times. This person understands the anxiety behind buying a home and will help you calm down.

- **Authority** – This person is loaded with knowledge about the market and inventory, understands the ins-and-outs of real estate, and is confident in that knowledge and experience. This person is a take-charge type.

- **Team** – This is a group of people who specialize in certain aspects of real estate, usually led by an authority (the face on all the promotional material). This team is on call at all hours – an efficient and effective, well-oiled machine. The only downside is you will never work with the person you met on your introductory visit (if you met him or her at all).

- **Legacy Broker** – This person is someone who has been the go-to person in a certain family or social circle. She ot he values the relationship with the larger group, so you know she or he won't steer you wrong. However, this kind of agent is difficult to find ... and it's hard to get inside that inner circle.

These categories aren't definitive. Every agent is probably a mixture of each. But hopefully this gives you a *general* idea of how agents can have different personalities and approaches.

*(Personally, I would say I'm probably more of the Authority, with a little hand holder mixed in when I'm dealing with clients. I tend to work well with people who have lots of questions such as first time homebuyers. – Paul)*

## 8. *Do* choose a full-time, seasoned REALTOR

When it comes to buying or selling a home, you want an experienced, professional real estate agent by your side. As we've said elsewhere in the book, you want an agent that eats, breathes, and sleeps real estate. Don't settle for a part-timer, and don't be someone else's learning curve!

Full time agents have a few distinctive traits that set them apart from part-timers.

- They are career real estate specialists

- They will work to lower your risk

- They will work for you at their own risk

- They understand the current market

- They have and know inventory

- They understand the complexity of the transaction

- They have *wisdom* versus just *knowledge.* Wisdom is the ability to apply years of knowledge. A rookie can have knowledge if they read a few books—it takes an experienced Realtor to truly have market **wisdom.**

In addition, look for agents with some additional training. Having various certifications doesn't guarantee an agent will be right for you (or even a good agent at all), but it at least shows that they are dedicated to professional development.

You'll know this when you see the weird acronyms behind their name. Here's what some of those acronyms mean:

- **CRS (Certified Residential Specialist)**: A network of 33,000 agents who receive tools and training to help buyers or sellers make the residential transaction as smooth as possible.

- **GRI (Graduate Realtor Institute)**: According to National Association of Realtors' website, GRI designees: *Have pursued a course of study that represents the minimum common body of knowledge for progressive real estate professionals, have developed a solid foundation of knowledge and skills to navigate the current real estate climate (no matter what the market condition), and act with professionalism and are committed to serving their clients and customers with the highest ethical standards.*

- **ABR (Accredited Buyer's Representative)**: Another designation that signals to buyers that a real estate agent is serious about honing their skills.

- **Certified *Realtor***: Many people mistakenly believe the term "Realtor" is synonymous with real estate agent. It is not. According to the NAR's website, *the term REALTOR® is a registered collective membership mark that identifies a real estate professional who is a member of the*

*NATIONAL ASSOCIATION of REALTORS® and subscribes to its strict **Code of Ethics**.*

*The Code establishes time-honored and baseline principles that come from the collective experiences of REALTORS® since the Code of Ethics was first established in 1913. Those principles can be loosely defined as:*

- *Loyalty to clients;*
- *Fiduciary (legal) duty to clients;*
- *Cooperation with competitors*
- *Truthfulness in statements and advertising*

There are many other designations and acronyms. Everything from resort specialists to working with senior citizens. If there is a niche market, it's safe to say there is probably a professional certification with a fancy acronym!

While agents *without* designations can be as superb as those *with* the designation, one thing you know that you are getting with an agent who has additional designations is a commitment to excellence and professional growth.

### 9. *Do* ask friends for referrals

Getting recommendations from friends is an essential step in finding a great real estate agent. But when asking, **be very**

**specific.** This is where most people go wrong in seeking referrals. Be extremely specific about what you are looking for in an agent! A simple question like, "Do you know any good agents?" won't cut it.

What your friends and family like in a real estate agent *may not be what you like*. To evaluate a recommendation, ask your friend or relative a few additional questions:

- What about this agent do you like?

- What was your experience working with this agent?

- What didn't you like about this agent?

- What do you wish they had done differently?

If you like what you hear, jump on the real estate agents' website and find out as much as you can about them. Feel free to visit them at an open house.

And again, we think it's extremely important for a real estate agent to have a public list of testimonials available. Testimonials are the only way of proving that past clients are *happy* clients. If they weren't, they wouldn't have agreed to do a testimonial! Some testimonials from Paul's clients can be found at *(have you figured out what Paul's website is yet? - T.J.)* www.gteamsellshomes.com.

## 10. *Do* choose an agent who responds to communication

How soon did he return your call? Did he return your call at all? Does he respond to text messages, emails, social media, or blog comments? For how long? This may seem minor, but how soon and how often an agent responds to your communication will tell you a lot about who he is and how he works.

Keep in mind that some agents will put their best foot forward when first meeting, so first impressions may be deceptive. Ask for some references, and then follow up with them to see what they thought about the agent's responsiveness.

Personally, we guarantee to all clients that we will stay in touch with them *a minimum of* once a week. Even if there is nothing new to report, you will hear from us!

One more thing—remember that YOU are in the driver's seat. YOU are in control. YOU are buying or selling a house……not the real estate agent. Don't let the real estate agent's agenda get in front of yours.

Paul met a woman who we will call "Mary" (not her real name.) Mary grew up on a farm in southern Anne Arundel County, and was a country girl at heart. The home she was raised in was an old 2-story home, with lots of character. The yard had many mature trees and a long winding driveway. *That's what she wanted.*

Unfortunately, her real estate agent was only showing her ramblers in town….and kept making strange comments like, "As we age we should make sure to have a main floor bedroom and a smaller yard." In fact, "Maybe you should just rent," the real estate agent told her.

Well, wouldn't ya know it…….it just so happened that this agent owned a rental property in town and badly needed a new tenant!

Mary was so discouraged and frustrated that she almost fell for it. Eventually, she found an agent who listened to her and what her dream was. Mary didn't care about a main floor bedroom. She could deal with that. Mary was also very independent and was very capable of handling a large yard and long driveway.

Moral of the story? Don't settle for someone else's idea of what's perfect for you. It's YOUR money. It's YOUR home. Follow YOUR dream!

# 8. First-Time Homebuyer? Six Things You MUST Do (That Most First-Time Homebuyers Completely Ignore)

Buying your first house can be scary.

It's a huge investment – quite possibly the biggest one you will ever make in your lifetime. And unless you grew up with parents who were real estate agents, you are probably a little intimidated by the whole process!

How do you know if you are buying the right house?

Who do you trust?

What do you need to know about your credit score?

When should you get pre-approved?

How much can you afford?

These are the kinds of questions that are probably racing through your mind right now. Hopefully, this book (and specifically this chapter) will help you navigate these unchartered waters….making your first home-buying experience pleasant and memorable.

And keep this in mind throughout the process: **it will be worth it to be a homeowner!**

**1. Check Your Credit Score**

Let's start from the top. You aren't going to be able to buy a home unless you have at least *pretty good* credit. It doesn't have to be perfect, but it can't be below average or mediocre. So, now is the time to clean it up before you start the home buying process!

What you *don't* want are a bunch of surprises showing up on your score down the road when you are ready to close on a house. This is a *badddddd* time to find out that your credit isn't what you thought it was! We've had homebuyers break down in tears (literally) when they found out their credit score prevented them from buying a home they had their heart set on.

It's better to take care of this right away so you don't have to worry about it when you actually start house hunting—even if you are absolutely certain your score is good. You never know what could be on it.

You can get a copy of your credit score from the three major credit agencies (or by talking to a local bank):

- Experian

- Equifax

- TransUnion

## 2. Evaluate Your Credit Cards

When it comes to credit cards, you need to think wisely about how you are using them. Many, many, many young people abuse their "plastic." Having bad habits with credit cards WILL prevent you from someday buying your first house. That's a fact.

Let that sink in!

This specifically haunts first time homebuyers, because they usually have a relatively low income. Because their expenses take up a larger chunk of that income, any additional credit card debt makes it difficult for a bank to justify loaning them money. They have a thin "margin" every month, and that scares potential lenders.

Typically, mortgage lenders don't want you to spend any more than 33% of your monthly income directly on housing. For example, if you're making $2,000/month, that equates to $660. When you add credit card debt (which usually has VERY HIGH interest rates) to the equation, banks will *not* approve your mortgage.

We're not saying you can't have *some* credit card debt— it completely depends on your various income/expenses/debt ratios. **Preferably you have zero debt, and you pay your credit card balance in full every single month.** But remember: the worst type of debt to have is high interest rate credit card debt

(which was probably used to buy unnecessary consumer goods like TV's, clothes, spring break vacations, etc.)

So the next time your friends are headed to Fells Point, a Ravens game, or are planning on dinner in Little Italy…..stay at home. It will feel weird at first, but you will soon get addicted to the emotional rush of saving money. As you pay down any debt you may have, you are one step closer to a better credit score……and your first home!

**There *are* amazing "first time homebuyer" mortgage programs out there, but you need to have solid finances!**

So before you even start *looking* at homes, get strategic about this. Read a Dave Ramsey book or two, and apply his advice. If you have outstanding credit card balances, pay them down to zero! Live extremely frugally, and make temporary lifestyle sacrifices.   Trust me—it will feel amazing when you have little to no credit card debt, and you're able to qualify for a home because of your above average credit score!

**3. Create a Budget**

Before you ever buy a house you should create a monthly budget based upon what you would pay *if you already owned a house.*

This exercise has a number of advantages. First, it teaches you to live within your housing budget when it isn't as risky to do so. Living for three or four months on a "restricted" budget will give you an idea of whether or not your expectations are realistic.

**In other words, it will teach you what you can truly afford.** Better to find out when you have the income than when you already have the house…..but don't have the money.

In our experience, many first time homebuyers buy a house that's at the top of their budget. They technically can afford it, but they have little to no money left over every month for entertainment, eating out, etc. It's no fun to live in your own home if you can't go to the movies once a month, eat out with your friends, etc.

Plan accordingly!

In addition, you'll be able to save more money toward a potential down payment (which you should have been building for a number of years by now), pay off any remaining debt (like credit cards or car loans), save money for any moving expenses, and build an emergency fund.

And if you don't already have a few thousand dollars in an emergency fund, you really shouldn't buy a house. Things *will* go wrong. A furnace could go out (not a fun thing during Baltimore winters), air conditioning could stop working, water leaks in the ceiling, siding repaired, or your car could break down.

You NEED to have some liquid cash available to pay for unforeseen "emergency" expenses.

The goal of this exercise is to pay above anything that you pay as a renter. So on top of your normal housing bills; start to pay an additional amount based upon items like:

- Home mortgage

- Homeowners Insurance

- Annual property taxes

- Home Owners Association fees

- Home furnishings

- Maintenance and repairs (even if you are moving into a new house, expect something to break down….because it will!)

- Cleaning

- Utilities

If you're currently renting, ask your landlord for all of the fees that he or she pays, and include those in your monthly budget. This budget is useful, too, when it actually comes time to make an offer on a home – you can present this budget to your lender for additional evidence that you can afford the loan since mortgage lenders like to see bank and credit card statements. Plus, it will give the lender confidence that you are a financially responsible adult that knows how to plan and budget.

Another thing to consider is special circumstances with your insurance policy. **Contact your insurance agent.** For example, we have run into problems with properties needing flood insurance in certain areas, *even if they aren't on the water!* The cost of flood insurance has killed a couple of deals we have had because it put the Customer over budget. This is just one example. So be sure to talk to your insurance agent beforehand!

Oh, and this is a great time to start collecting pay stubs and all financial statements in a folder that you will keep current as new information comes through the door!

### 4. Find a Lender AND GET PREAPPROVED

Next to your real estate agent, the mortgage lender is the other most important professional you'll want to meet when it comes to buying a new home. A good real estate agent can introduce you to a good lender.

How do you spot a good lender? *(I'll give you a hint; he's tall, handsome and the co-author of this book! – T.J.)* Our best advice? Do not go to a website like Lending Tree © unless you want 10 -15 calls a day for the next month asking you about getting a mortgage. Make sure your lender understands and can demonstrate the immediate, short term, & long term cost of various mortgage programs. T.J. uses an advanced analytical program that will compare up to 5 different mortgages for your review.  This allows you to make an educated choice about what is best for you – not your lender.

**Don't allow anyone to run your credit score until you've picked a lender.** If several people try to access your score over a short period of time, your credit score can suffer.

By the way, avoid choosing a lender based on "points" (especially if we are talking about just an eighth or a quarter.) In fact, you might be tempted to work with an online lender because of low interest rates. DON'T.  Online lenders – and their underwriters – are usually hard to contact and are not in control of the situation.

You'll just have to trust us on this one—you would much rather work with a lender that is a great communicator, is trustworthy, and is responsive to your needs than a lender who is none of those things……but offers a slightly lower interest rate.

If you're a first time homebuyer, you may even want to take a little higher of a rate and allow the lender to pay some of your closing costs.  A difference of quarter a percent on a $175,000 home won't make that much of a difference on your

Good agents can also help you bid if things become competitive, and bargain with the seller to get a fair price. This is especially true if they are requesting buyers without inspection or appraisal contingencies—*two things that will be the first to be dropped if you are in a competitive market.* That can be disconcerting figuring you may put an offer on a house that might not pass inspection or appraise for less than you are offering. In a seller's market, a good buyer's agent is CRUCIAL.

We've written extensively in this book about how to choose the *right* real estate agent. Make sure you read it cover to cover!

**6. Be Ready**

Once you've evaluated your credit score, worked on a new budget, contacted a real estate agent, and found a lender, it's *now* time to start looking at houses.

<u>Unfortunately, most first time homebuyers do NONE of these things.</u>

They immediately go online and start looking for homes. Some even start driving around to check out properties they found online. This is a HUGE mistake, because you have absolutely no idea what you qualify for, what you can afford, etc.

Hopefully this chapter convinces you to "take care of business" *before* you actually start house hunting!

If you are in a seller's market, you'll now understand why I recommend that you do everything above *first*: you must be ready to pounce on a great house when you find it. In hot markets, every day matters. Heck, sometimes every *hour* matters.

If you don't have your down payment, budget, and pre-approval, you might miss out on the perfect home.

And it's important during this time (it could take anywhere from three to six months) to keep your financial record *clean*. Don't make any major purchases, and keep on top of your bills. **One of the biggest mistakes we've seen is buying a car prior to applying for a mortgage.** Unless your income has gone up significantly since you financed your car, it will be very difficult to qualify for a mortgage if you already have monthly car payment obligations. So if you're driving a nicer, newer car, ask yourself if you'd rather have *that,* or own a home. Chances are you'd be better off driving a reliable used car, and putting the difference towards your dream of owning a home.

So, again, don't make any major purchases before applying for mortgage pre-approval. You don't want that final look at your finances to be disrupted.

And before you actually make an offer on a house, do the following:

- Call the utility providers (electric, water, sewer, garbage) to find out average monthly billing

- Find out about any potential homeowner association fees

- Look at the property taxes

Now, add all of those extra expenses to your budget, and ask yourself an honest question: **can you *still* afford the house?**

Here's the bottom line: don't fall for a beautiful home if the expenses are going to drive you over your budget. Don't let anyone push you to go into the upper ends of your budget…or over your budget. Even if you could technically afford the house, if you don't have any money left over, you are not going to be able to take care of the house!

**Also avoid spending all your available cash on the down payment and closing costs.** Otherwise, if you run into emergency repairs and unexpected costs, you will have to ask your parents to bail you out…….because the bank will not.

# 9. Should You Sell Your Home Without An Agent? Insider Tips For Marketing Your Home As A "For Sale By Owner"

The easiest way to teach is through stories. Here's a story to tell my point.

"Cheryl" had a home in Perry Hall. (Cheryl is not her real name.) She had a **For Sale By Owner** sign in her yard. Paul introduced himself and asked if he could help her. She literally chased him off the property, saying "real estate agents are thieves," and that she was selling it herself.

Hey - everyone is entitled to their opinion, we just don't agree with hers!

A couple of weeks later Paul was in the neighborhood and decided to drive by and see if she was still trying to sell the home on her own.....and saw a moving truck!

"Good for her," Paul said to himself, "she must have gotten lucky and found the perfect buyer."

Paul knew Cheryl's neighbor (which is how he originally found out about the property,) so he stopped in to speak with him. He said that she had in fact sold the house. Now, Paul knew that this house *should have* sold for around $260,000 at that time. Usually FSBO listings don't get full market value, so he was guessing she had accepted a lowball offer for her to have gotten such a quick sale. Maybe $220k or $230k.

Boy was he was wrong.

She sold it, all by herself, for.....**$128,000!!!** We wish we were kidding. We can't make stuff like this up. Think of how long it would take to save up the difference between what her home was actually worth and what she sold it for. She flushed a lifetime of savings down the toilet. What a tragedy! We suppose she avoided capital gains taxes, if that's any consolation.

Now, obviously this is an extreme (yet true) example of what can happen when you try to do it "on your own." Not everyone will make a mistake this costly. But you should be aware of the risks!

For sale by owners have a reputation in our industry. Amongst real estate agents, we even have a slang term for them: "FSBO's," pronounced *fizzbo's*.

As in the "fizz" created by soda pop, and "bows" used to fire arrows.

Fizzbo's.

There are typically two main reasons homeowners

decide to sell their home *without* using a licensed real estate agent.

1. They want to save $$$ on the commission because they feel they can do it themselves (cut out the middleman)
1. They originally listed their home with a licensed real estate agent, but are disappointed with the agent's mediocre performance/marketing plan

**Here's what you should know:** over 84% of FSBO's eventually list with a licensed real estate agent. It's almost inevitable.

Why?

Sellers soon realize that selling a $200,000 product (or whatever price the home is listed at) is not as easy as pounding a sign into the yard and waiting for the phone to ring. And even in hot markets where that can work, it's almost a full time job responding to the phone calls, requests for tours, etc. If the seller has a fulltime job or other time commitments, this makes things *extremely* difficult.

And in our modern age, we think a major reason that many homeowners try to "cut out the middleman" and avoid using a real estate agent can be summed up in one phrase: **the Internet.**

People mistakenly believe that homes are commodities. They think to themselves, "I'll just take a few pictures, write a paragraph or two about the features, upload it to a local *For Sale By Owner* website, and wait for the phone to ring!"

And then they wait.

And wait.

And wait.

The phone never rings. If it does, potential buyers are usually looking to score a great deal. They throw out lowball offers. And we can't blame them.

Here's why: when your home is listed as a "For Sale By Owner," **the buyer knows that there isn't a middleman.**

They feel that *they* are entitled to some of that extra profit—not you, the seller. So typically they make lower offers than they otherwise would. This practically eliminates any hypothetical "savings" that may have been realized.......if the home is lucky enough to attract any offers to begin with. In fact, many homes listed without an agent fail to attract a single offer or phone call.

When this inevitably happens, the seller gets frustrated. *Very* frustrated (and understandably so).

Eventually, months later, he or she will end up listing the house with a licensed agent.

We won't beat around the bush here—we firmly believe it is in your best interest to buy and sell real estate with an experienced, licensed agent (preferably a certified Realtor.)

But……

If you're dead set on selling your home *without* a real estate agent, we want to share some insider secrets with you. We've made it super easy—just go online to a free information website we created for Baltimore area *For Sale By Owner* listings:

www.BaltimoreFSBOinsider.com

Once you've gone to BaltimoreFSBOinsider.com, you will find lots of helpful tools that will come in handy if you decide to sell your home without an agent. Again, while we don't recommend it, we *do* want you to be successful.

We are offering —free of charge—a marketing system designed *exclusively* for FSBO listings (you will have to use some different tactics than a regular real estate agent would, because you will not have access to the MLS distribution network.)

**Oh, and one more thing…..did you know that there's a way to list your home with a licensed real estate agent and still not pay any commission when it sells?** It's a sort of "hybrid" listing trick that combines the best of both worlds.

We reveal this secret at BaltimoreFSBOinsider.com!

Trust us on this one…..if you're even *remotely considering* trying to sell your house on your own, you NEED to know about this! In fact, at the risk of offending some people, we would even say you'd be crazy *not to* find out more.

We've been in this business for many years—we know what works and what won't!

The two of us have successfully completed numerous transactions (many of them were homes that were listed with Paul's team because they originally failed to sell as a *FSBO*,) and we're confident that this information will empower you to do it right the first time.

When it comes to real estate, mistakes can be really expensive. I want you to learn from my experience!

This information will be INCREDIBLY valuable if and when you decide to sell your home without a real estate agent.

Again, everything you need to know can be found at **baltimoreFSBOinsider.com.**

Good luck!

# 10. What Is Title Insurance and Why Do I Need It?

## Most homebuyers are surprised to find that title insurance could save them hundreds of thousands of dollars…..And here's how!

By Robert Selznick

*Senior Account Manager*, All Star Title, Inc.

6225 Smith Ave., Suite 202

Baltimore, MD 21209

Phone: 800-580-0677

www.allstartitle.com

Purchasing a home can be a very overwhelming process for many buyers, especially for first time homebuyers. You are handed stacks of papers to sign and between the purchase contract and lender's documents, you may be forced to become ambidextrous when it comes to signing your name. Eventually, you will make your way to the summary of costs associated with your loan and notice that you are paying for two types of title insurance policies. These fees can appear costly and you may not even know what you are protecting yourself against.

What is title insurance? Do I need it? What does it protect me from?

Not only am I going to explain the answers to these questions, but I'm also going to give you a real life example of how purchasing owner's title insurance saved one couple tens of thousands of dollars.

So, what exactly is title insurance? The formal definition states, "Insurance against loss due to an unknown defect in a title or interest in real estate". To simplify that further, title insurance is your monetary protection against someone making a claim to your home. When you purchase your home, there are two title insurance policies offered to you. One is called "Lender's Title Insurance" (this is required by all lenders to be purchased) and the other is "Owner's Title Insurance" (this is optional). The difference between the two is very simple. The former protects the lender in the case of a claim and the latter protects the homebuyer.

Many people have the misconception that title insurance protects them from losing their home in the event of a rightful title claim. This is, however, not the case. The insurance protects the monetary investment made. For example, if you were to opt out of the owner's policy and a successful claim was made, your lender would be protected on the money that was lent to you for the purchase. You, however, would be out any down payment and accrued equity on top of losing your home. So the answer to our second question, "Do I need it?" is a very simple, YES. Being that an Owner's Title Policy, a one-time upfront fee, is only several more hundred dollars in addition to the Lender's Policy that is required, I can't see where the benefit of not purchasing outweighs the risk. You also have the peace of mind that the protection remains as long as you or your heirs have an interest in the property.

The final question many homebuyers may have is "What does this protect me from?" There is a laundry list of potential reasons for a title claim, but I want to outline some of the most common.

- Forged Deeds, Financial and Property Records
- Unknown Heirs with Claims Against the Property
- Public Property Record Errors
- Unknown Property Liens
- Undisclosed Encumbrances
- Property Easements

Now if you are still awake, I'd like to give a real life example of how purchasing an Owner's Policy saved one couple over $15,000!

## Forgery and Infidelity

Fraud is one of the most common causes of title claims and can be almost impossible for a title agent to know about until after the fact. In this case, the homebuyers made a costly mistake by not purchasing an Owner's Policy.

In 2001, Paul and Sharon purchased a home together and took title to the property as join tenants. In 2005, Sharon moved out of the home after learning of Paul's infidelity. The following year, Paul decided to sell the property without Sharon's knowledge. He showed up to the closing table and presented the settlement attorney with a specific, full authority power of attorney signed by Sharon and properly executed and sealed by a Notary Public. Using the power of attorney, Paul signed the closing documents for his self and on behalf of Sharon; including the deed and a disbursement authorization that directed all the sales proceeds to be wired into his personal savings account. In 2011, the homebuyers were served with a lawsuit brought by Sharon and her attorney claiming her interest in the property. It turned out that Sharon's signature on the power of attorney document presented at the closing had been forged and that Notary Public was complicit in the fraud. The homebuyers spent over $15,000 in attorney fees defending their title to the property. Had they purchased an Owner's Policy, those costs would have been covered by the title insurance. Should the homebuyer's wind up losing the home as well, they will also lose any money invested to buy the property as well as any money used to make improvements to the home.

## Conclusion

Hopefully this true story reveal an important truth: Owner's Title Insurance not only protects you from actual financial loss caused by a covered title problem, but also provides the same protection to your heirs for so long as they may own the property. It even covers the full cost of defending you against such covered claims!

**A one-time premium provides all of this coverage on the largest single investment you may ever make.**

Nothing else guarantees a homebuyer peace of mind quite like title insurance.

Our goal at *All Star Title, Inc.* is to provide unparalleled value for both you and your customers.

3. **We will close any time, any where!**
4. **Competitive Fees:** We will match or beat any competitor offer
5. **Mail away closings** for clients out of state. We even do international.
6. **Hectic customer schedules?** Separate closings for Buyers and sellers available.
7. **New website** with features and FAQ's at www.allstartitle.com

***Okay, this is Paul and Tom again***—We just wanted to say that it is extremely important that you invest in title insurance. We <u>cannot emphasize this enough</u>. Do NOT invest hundreds of thousands of dollars on any type of real estate without proper title insurance. Hopefully the stories Rob shared convinced you of this! Seriously people…..INVEST IN TITLE INSURANCE!

# 11. BONUS CHAPTER: Think Your House Is Ready For The Market? Here's Why "Staging" Will Help Your Home Sell Faster....For A Higher Price!

By Kevin Hogan

Licensed Realtor, Professional Stager

kevinwaltonhogan@hotmail.com

443-536-9966

*Time and money*......two things most of us wish we had **more** of, right?

*Work and stress*, two things most of us wish we had **less** of, right?

When it comes to selling a house, these realities may become foremost in our minds. If there was ever a time you needed professional expertise to help you through a process…..this is it.

A Realtor who is knowledgeable in the market, knows what is selling and for how much, **and** knows how to look at the house with "buyers eyes," and see exactly what should be done *before* listing, can save you time, money, work and stress.

After writing the listing agreement, a competent Realtor will advertise your property, schedule showings with your approval, provide the necessary forms, represent you in negotiating a contract for purchase, show you what your expected net proceeds will be, keep you constantly informed of all activity on your property, and can arrange for closing services.

If time is an issue (as it should be, after all, time is money), **getting a house ready for market is crucial.** Grab those first lookers, because they knew enough about the property to be interested in scheduling a showing! They most likely have seen it online (about 90% of buyers shop online first). They liked the photos, know the square footage, room layout, etc....so when they step into the door, make sure they know this is the house they've been looking for! It should be appealing and welcoming.

A Realtor needs to know how to make a house appeal to the senses. Most sellers need help in reaching that point and *most* Realtors (not all) don't know or don't want to risk offending clients and losing the listing.......so they are reluctant to offer staging advice.

One of my very first listings resulted from a seller who called me after his 6 month listing expired with another agency, telling me he had asked the listing agent, "What can we do to help our house show better?"

The other agent had told him the house was fine! I could, however, see a lot of room for improvement. I was able to give him a very do-able list that he and his wife promptly dug into, spending less than $500 total. It resulted in a sale to the very next buyers who were shown the house. They were thrilled and remarked, "I wish we had called you 6 months ago!"

Of course, not all staging projects will be that inexpensive. In fact, the national average spent on staging a house is about 1-3% of the list price. How well the house has been maintained is a huge factor, if the roof or basement leaks, those types of issues obviously are a higher priority than painting and redecorating.

It is important to remember that *staging is not covering up problems!*

Often, Realtors will provide the seller with a beginning list price and ask them to consider a price reduction if there are no offers within 30 days. This price reduction can be substantial **and unnecessary** if part of that money is spent up front on presenting the property at its best and making sure that the original price is on target and not unrealistically bumped up to impress the sellers and secure the listing.

This is a fact: every home (except one) that I have staged, aside from my own properties, has already been on the market for a considerable amount of time. **And every home that I have staged has sold, as far as I know.**

The exception is a property on Green Lake whose owner called me to stage *before* listing (smart move!), and during the low point of the housing market in our area this lake home still sold. The owner still expresses his appreciation every time I see him. I love that!

## Understanding the importance of thoughtful preparation

It should be your agents mission to protect and enhance the equity position of your house by implementing property preparation strategies which have been proven to increase the sales price and reduce days a property will remain on the market.

By using unbiased proven procedures a Staging Professional can analyze each impression area of your property and make suggestions which are guaranteed to increase the sales price and reduce the days on the market.

A Staging analysis will allow you to see the property through the eyes of the buyer, giving you the tools to enhance your properties sale price and reduce the days that your home will remain for sale on the market.

Without the skills to properly prepare a home for the competitive marketplace you are leaving money at the closing table. This can be the difference between a nice profit on the sale of your home and just breaking even. Today, market preparation is one of the most important steps to ensure retail sales price and the least amount of time on the market.

There are many low and no cost decisions which will prepare your property to make a strong emotional connection with the widest cross section of today's buyers. These are the strategies being employed by our nation's most profitable builders, developers and property managers to get the highest possible price in the least amount of time.

One example is Lightening and Brightening your home by spending $80 to $100 can increase the sales price by 800%. In other words if you spend $100 you can add $800 to your sale price. Another is making your bathroom spotless with $10 worth of caulk and cleaners; shiny tile, sparkling mirrors, clean grout lines & fresh caulk are on every buyers wish list!

Even something as simple as putting down fresh mulch and making sure the lawn is mowed and the yard free of clutter can net you an extra $1000 or more, in addition to putting the potential buyer in the right frame of mind before they even step foot inside the door.

Of course we sometimes have to spend a little more money to do things like replace carpet or paint. This is often because of odors that have permeated the house. Odor is the number one deterrent in procuring the initial emotional connection necessary to engage your buyers interest.

"The" first and lasting impression on your potential buyer is heavy scent. As they enter your home. PET ODOR, SMOKING, KITTY LITTER, OILY COOKING, OVERBEARING DEODORIZERS trying to mask all of the above are potential deal breakers. A fresh coat of paint and new carpet or wood-laminate will often eliminate odor besides giving your house a 'new' feeling.

## Staging Statistics

*The National Association of Realtors* states that those who generally spend 1-3% of the value of their home preparing their home to sell (staging), reap 6-13% in average price value (fewer price reductions, carrying costs, or home sitting on the market) and a 40% faster sale. Wow!

**Your Home's "Staging Potential" at 1%:_____ = 8%_____ in Average Price Value**

This formula shows that using *conservative* figures, if your home is worth $500,000 and you spend 1% to stage it - $5000 (this figure includes much more than staging fees, this includes new furniture, paying electricians, painters, and carpenters if needed)….you will then expect an 8% return on your investment. Which is $40,000!

Statistics show that staging your home for sale will shorten your "Days on Market" and bring you a higher price for your home. Period.

## *BUYERS*?

What about buyers? As important as it is for Realtors and their sellers to know about proper staging, it is equally important for a Realtor to know what problems or potential problems to look for in a house when helping prospective buyers.

As emphasized elsewhere in this book, a buyer's agent will make sure that there is a home inspection contingency included in a purchase agreement, have knowledge and experience in home construction and maintenance, *and* be well equipped to negotiate with the sellers' agent after any issues are discovered during the home inspection.

An ethical and experienced Realtor will know when to advise their buyers to walk away from the home they *thought* they wanted, even though it might mean more work for the Realtor to get the sale and commission check they are hoping for!

# Dedications

### Richard Kwolek

Richard was my (Paul's) stepfather, friend and golf buddy. Richard was a very vital part of my growth and development as a young man. He was a larger then life, misunderstood guy with a heart of gold. He always told me I would be successful in spite of my actions and popular opinion at the time. He saw it before anyone else. He saw it in me and told me I could be wildly successful and tried to show me the finer things in life. Richard passed away the very day that I received my first ratified contract in real estate. He is with me everyday and I try to convey good on his behalf daily. I will never forget the life lessons that he taught me. My only wish is that I had a chance to express the profound impact he had on my life. To Richard I dedicate this book. I hope that you are hitting the golf ball well in the fairways of heaven.

Paul Gillespie

"This book is dedicated to every person, young or old, blue collar or white collar, financially savvy or starting over again, experienced home owner or first time buyer that believes in the power of homeownership. You are the foundation of the U.S. economy. Without you, there would be no American Dream. I also dedicate this book to Kristy, Sydney, and Cameron Barker. I am who I am and do what I do because of the three of you."

-TJB

Made in the USA
Charleston, SC
04 September 2014